David Copperfield

Oxford Progressive English Readers provide a wide range of enjoyable reading at six language levels. Text lengths range from 8,000 words at the Starter level, to about 35,000 words at Level 5. The latest methods of text analysis, using specially designed software, ensure that readability is carefully controlled.

The aim of the series is to present stories to engage the interest of the reader; to intrigue, mystify, amuse, delight and stimulate the imagination.

David Copperfield

Charles Dickens

OXFORD
UNIVERSITY PRESS

OXFORD
UNIVERSITY PRESS

Oxford University Press is a department of the University of Oxford.
It furthers the University's objective of excellence in research, scholarship,
and education by publishing worldwide in

Oxford New York

Auckland Bangkok Buenos Aires Cape Town Chennai
Dar es Salaam Delhi Hong Kong Istanbul Karachi Kolkata
Kuala Lumpur Madrid Melbourne Mexico City Mumbai Nairobi
São Paulo Shanghai Singapore Taipei Tokyo Toronto

and an associated company in Berlin

Oxford is a registered trade mark of Oxford University Press

© Oxford University Press 2005

First published 1992

Second edition published 2005

This impression (lowest digit)

1 3 5 7 9 11 13 15 14 12 10 8 6 4 2

Illustrated by Choy Man Yung

Syllabus design and text analysis by David Foulds

0 19 597140 X

Printed in Hong Kong
Published by Oxford University Press (China) Ltd
18th Floor, Warwick House East, Taikoo Place, 979 King's Road, Quarry Bay
Hong Kong

Contents

Introduction

'Of all my books, I like this the best ... like many fond parents, I have in my heart of hearts a favourite child. And his name is DAVID COPPERFIELD.'

Charles Dickens, Preface to *David Copperfield*

Among the fifteen novels Charles Dickens wrote, *David Copperfield* was his favourite and was based on his own life. The story is set in the 1800s in England, where Dickens lived.

The story is written in the first person. An older David Copperfield tells what he remembers of his life, from the time as a young boy under the care of his mother until he has his own family. David meets a lot of people as he grows up, studies, and works. Some people are very cruel to him. But fortunately, he also meets some very nice people, who make his life happier. Apart from telling us about himself, David tells us how his friends have changed.

Important people in the story

The main character is David Copperfield, who was born into an unfortunate family. He has been looked after by Peggotty, the servant of his family, Mr Murdstone, his stepfather, and Betsy Trotwood, his aunt.

One of David's childhood friends is Emily, a girl who stays with Peggotty's family near the sea. Tommy Traddles and James Steerforth are his friends from his first school, Salem House.

Later, Betsy Trotwood's friend Mr Wickfield introduces David to another school. He makes friends with Agnes, the daughter of Mr Wickfield, and meets Uriah Heep, a young man who works for Mr Wickfield.

When he has finished school, David starts working for Mr Spenlow. There he meets Dora, Mr Spenlow's beautiful daughter.

About Charles Dickens

Charles Dickens was a very popular writer who lived in England in the nineteenth century. He was born in 1812 in Landport and spent his childhood in Kent. He had seven brothers and sisters and he was the second child in the family. His father had many debts and was put in prison when Charles was about twelve. Charles Dickens had to earn money for his family by working at his relative's factory, labelling bottles for six shillings a week. He attended a day school at the same time. Two years later, he left school and worked at a lawyer's office. He taught himself shorthand when he was sixteen because he wanted to be a reporter. At nineteen he became one of the quickest and most accurate reporters in London. Later, he worked as an editor and a writer.

Dickens never stopped writing after he published his first novel, *The Pickwick Papers* in 1836–37. Usually he published a chapter of a novel every month. He wrote fifteen novels in total, the most popular ones include *Oliver Twist, A Christmas Carol, David Copperfield, A Tale of Two Cities* and *Great Expectations.* His own favourite novel was *David Copperfield*, in which his own life is reflected.

Dickens spent most of his life in London. He died of a stroke in 1870 and was buried in Westminster Abbey.

1
An Unhappy Childhood

Early memories

The first people I can remember in my life are my
mother and our servant, Peggotty. I did not know
my father at all. He had died before I was born.

My mother had pretty hair and a lovely shape, but 5
Peggotty had no shape at all. Her arms were very hard
and her cheeks were as red as apples. I was surprised
the birds did not come and try to eat her.

I can still remember our house, with the bedroom
windows open to let the fresh air in. There was a 10
garden, with a high fence round it. I remember seeing
butterflies, and fruit trees. The fruit on these trees was
riper and sweeter than any I have known since, in any
other garden. Sometimes on cold evenings we played
games in front of the fire in the sitting room. I 15
remember my mother, out of breath, resting in a chair
and twisting the ends of her hair round her fingers. I
knew how proud she was of being
so pretty.

Peggotty and I were sitting
one night by the fire, alone.
I was reading to Peggotty
when the bell rang. We
went to the door. My
mother was there,
looking especially
pretty. With her
was a gentleman.

My mother bent down to take me in her arms and kiss me. The gentleman put his hand on my head; somehow I didn't like him. When he touched my hand he also touched my mother's hand, which was holding
5 me. I was jealous.

My mother thanked the gentleman for bringing her home. Then Peggotty shut the door and we all went into the sitting room.

Gradually I got used to seeing this gentleman, but I
10 never liked him. His name was Mr Murdstone.

One evening, about two months afterwards, Peggotty and I were together in the sitting room; my mother was out again. Peggotty said suddenly, 'Master Davy, would you like to go with me to Yarmouth? I am going to stay
15 for two weeks with my brother. There is the sea; and the boats and ships; and the fishermen; and the beach; and my nephew Ham to play with.'

I replied that it would be great fun.

The day for our journey to Yarmouth soon arrived.
20 We travelled in a farmer's cart, leaving in the morning after breakfast.

Just as we were going, my mother ran out to the gate. She called out to us to stop so she could kiss me. I cried and my mother cried too.

25 We left her standing by the garden gate. Then I saw Mr Murdstone coming along the road to our house. He spoke to my mother, and seemed to be angry with her for crying. I was looking back round the side of the cart. I wondered why he interfered, and Peggotty seemed to
30 wonder also.

A holiday

I was quite tired, and very glad, when we reached Yarmouth. Peggotty's nephew, Ham, was waiting for us there. Ham was a huge, strong man. He was six feet tall, but his young face made him look quite like a boy.

Ham carried me home on his back. After a while we came to a piece of low, flat ground. Ham said, 'There is our house, Master Davy!'

I looked all around me as far as I could see. There was no house anywhere.

Then, not far away, I saw an old black boat pulled up on dry ground. It had an iron pipe sticking out of it for a chimney. The smoke from this chimney made it look very warm and comfortable. 'Is that it?' said I. 'That thing like a ship?'

'That's it, Master Davy,' replied Ham.

The idea of living in a real boat delighted me. There was a door on one side, and little windows. To me, it seemed a perfect place to live in.

Waiting for us at the door were a sad-looking woman, and a most beautiful little girl. The little girl would not let me kiss her when I offered to. Instead she ran away and hid. Her name was Emily.

A little later, when we were having our dinner, a man came in. He had long, untidy hair and a pleasant face. He was Peggotty's brother, Mr Peggotty.

Later Peggotty told me that Ham and Emily were cousins, and Mr Peggotty was their uncle. Ham's parents had died, and so had Emily's. Mr Peggotty cared for both of them. The sad-looking woman, Mrs Gummidge, was the wife of Mr Peggotty's partner in a fishing boat. The partner had been drowned in a storm at sea. Mrs Gummidge was very poor, so Mr Peggotty cared for her, too, now.

That night, as I went to sleep, I heard the noise of the wind roaring out at sea, and the waves thundering on the shore. I was glad Mr Peggotty was there to look after us all.

In the morning it was bright and sunny. I got out of bed and went with little Emily to pick up stones on the beach.

'You like sailing, I suppose?' I said to Emily.

'No,' replied Emily, shaking her head, 'I'm afraid of the sea.'

'Afraid!' I said, looking at the sea bravely. 'I'm not!'

'Oh! But it is so cruel,' said Emily. 'I have seen it break a boat as big as our house.'

Of course, I was in love with Emily. We used to walk and play on the beach all day. In the evenings we sat together near the fire. I told Emily how much I loved her. She said she loved me, and I am sure she did.

At last the day came for me to leave, and when I returned home I found that there had been great changes. My mother had married Mr Murdstone, and he was now my father.

Mr Murdstone loved my mother very much, but he was not a kind man. 'David,' he said to me one day, 'if my horse or dog is disobedient, I beat him. I beat him hard. I say to myself "I'll defeat him," and I am determined to do it.' I knew then that Mr Murdstone would beat me if I displeased him.

One evening soon afterwards, Mr Murdstone's elder sister, Miss Murdstone, arrived. She was a cross-looking woman, with dark hair like her brother's. She had come to help my mother look after our home, and she would stay with us for always.

Lessons

Mr and Miss Murdstone had been talking about sending me away to school. They made my mother agree with their plans. In the meantime, I learnt lessons at home.

I shall never forget those lessons! I can still remember what they were like. My mother was supposed to teach me, but in fact the lessons were given by Mr Murdstone and his sister. They were always there. They pretended to be busy, but really they were waiting to interfere. The sight of these two frightened me so much that I forgot everything I had tried to learn.

It was always the same. Every evening I read some lessons in my lesson books. Each morning, after breakfast, I handed the books to my mother and began to tell her all that I could remember. But I could never do it without making mistakes. At the first mistake Mr Murdstone looked up. At the next mistake Miss Murdstone looked up. My face was red with shame. After several more mistakes I stopped. My mother dared not help me. She just said, softly, 'Oh Davy, Davy!'

'Now, Clara,' Mr Murdstone said, 'control the boy. Don't say, "Oh Davy, Davy!" Either he knows his lesson, or he does not know it.'

'He does not know it,' Miss Murdstone interrupted unpleasantly.

One morning, when I went into the sitting room as usual, I found my mother looking anxious and Miss Murdstone looking cross. Mr Murdstone was tying something round the end of a thin stick.

'I tell you, Clara,'
said Mr Murdstone,
'I was often beaten
myself when I was a child.'

5   I began the lesson badly, and went on worse. I was
so frightened by what Mr Murdstone had said that I
could not remember anything. At last my mother began
to cry.

'Clara!' Mr Murdstone warned.

10   I saw him give a signal to his sister. He got up,
picking up the stick.

'David, you and I will go upstairs, boy.'

He led me up to my room slowly. Then he suddenly
twisted my head under his arm, and struck me hard
15   with the cane. In the same instant, I seized the hand
which held me, between my teeth, and bit into it.

He beat me then as if he wished to kill me. I heard
my mother's cries — and Peggotty's. Then he left me,
and locked the door outside.

I was kept in this prison for five days. I saw no one but Miss Murdstone the whole time.

On the fifth night I was woken up by a noise. I sat up in bed, frightened. Then I realized someone on the other side of the door was calling my name. I got up.

Standing by the door, in the darkness, I whispered, 'Is that Peggotty?'

'Yes, my dear, precious Davy,' she replied.

'How is Mother, dear Peggotty? Is she very angry with me?'

I could hear Peggotty crying very softly on her side of the door, before she answered, 'No, not very.'

'What are they going to do with me, Peggotty dear?'

'School. Salem House. Near London,' was Peggotty's answer. 'Tomorrow!'

Then she whispered, 'Davy dear, I want to say something to you. I don't know what is going to happen, now. But you must never forget me. I will look after your mother as faithfully as I have looked after you.'

'Thank you, dear Peggotty! Oh, thank you!'

In the morning Miss Murdstone came in, and told me about going to school, but it was not such surprising news as she thought. She also told me to dress, come downstairs, and have my breakfast.

In the sitting room I saw my mother, looking very pale, and with red eyes. They had persuaded her to believe that I was a wicked child. She was more sorry about my wickedness than about losing me. This made me very sad.

2
Away from Home

Salem House

Soon after this the carriage came to the door. I looked for Peggotty, but she did not seem to be at home; nor was Mr Murdstone.

As my luggage was lifted into the carriage, my mother held me close to her. 'Goodbye, Davy. School will be good for you. I forgive you, my dear boy. God will protect you.'

'Clara!' warned Miss Murdstone.

Miss Murdstone went with me to the carriage, and I got in. We began to move away from my home, and soon after that my handkerchief was completely wet with tears.

Suddenly, after about half a mile, the carriage stopped.

To my great surprise, Peggotty climbed into the carriage. She seized me in both her arms and squeezed me. Then she brought out some cakes, and pushed them into my pocket. Still not saying a word, she took out a purse which she put into my hand. She gave me a last squeeze, got down from the carriage and hurried away.

The purse had three bright silver coins in it, which I could see Peggotty had polished until they shone. But it contained something else, even more precious to me — two more coins, larger than the others, folded in a bit of paper; and on the paper, in my mother's writing, were the words, 'For Davy. With my love.'

The carriage stopped at Yarmouth. There, after a quick meal, I got into a larger carriage and began my journey to London.

When I saw London in the distance I was excited and curious. Gradually we came nearer to it, and finally arrived at the little hotel where the carriage stopped.

I felt very lonely as I got down from the carriage and went into the office. No one had come to meet me. No one seemed to know what to do with me. I sat down and began to think: perhaps Mr Murdstone had planned to lose me in London. What would happen if I tried to walk home? Would anyone there, besides Peggotty, welcome me?

But then a tall, thin young man, dressed in a black suit, entered and whispered to the clerk. I noticed that his suit was rather short in the sleeves and legs.

'Are you the new boy?' he said to me.

I thought I must be, but didn't know.

'I am one of the masters at Salem House School,' he said. 'My name is Mr Mell.'

'Please, sir,' I said, 'is the school far from here?'

'About six miles. We shall go by carriage.'

Salem House was a square brick building. It looked empty. It was so quiet that I thought the boys must have gone out. However, Mr Mell told me that it was holiday time and all the boys were at home. He seemed surprised that I did not know. Mr Creakle, the owner of the school, had gone to the seaside with his wife and daughter. I discovered that I had been sent there in holiday time as a punishment for my bad behaviour. There would be no lessons, and no other boys in the school, for four weeks.

Mr Mell took me to see a classroom, and left me there by myself. I thought it was a sad and lonely place. I stared at the long rows of desks and the old writing books which were lying on the dirty floor. Walking quietly to the end of the long room I suddenly saw a cardboard notice lying on a desk. It said, 'Be careful. He bites.'

5   I thought there might be a large dog somewhere in the room. I was frightened and climbed on top of the desk.

    When Mr Mell came back he asked me why I was standing up there.

10   'Excuse me, sir,' I said, 'I'm looking for the dog.'

    'Dog?' he said. 'Which dog?'

    'The one that bites.'

    'No, Copperfield,' he said sadly, 'that notice doesn't refer to a dog. It refers to a boy. I have to put this notice 15 on your back, Copperfield. I am sorry to do this, but I must.'

The notice

He lifted me off the desk and tied the notice on my shoulders. Everywhere I went I had to wear it.

20   No one knew how much I suffered. Whether people could see me or not, I always imagined that somebody was reading that piece of cardboard. Soon there would be forty-five boys in the school, and I imagined all of them crying out in their different voices, 'Be careful. He 25 bites.'

    After about a month Mr Creakle returned. I was ordered to go to his room before I went to bed that evening. When I saw him I was very frightened.

    Mr Creakle was a fat gentleman with a bunch of keys 30 and a watch on a chain. He was sitting in a large chair with a glass and a bottle beside him. He had a red face which made him look very angry, and small eyes deep in his head; a little nose and a large chin. He had some

thin hair that looked wet, brushed over the sides of his
head, but none on the top. However, there was one
thing about Mr Creakle that frightened me more than
his appearance — he had no voice.
He only spoke in a whisper.   5

Mr Creakle wanted to
tell me that he was a
determined man, like my
father, Mr Murdstone,
and that he would
make me obey him.

'When I tell
someone to do a
thing, I make them
do it,' he whispered   15
at me, pinching my
ear fiercely.

I was very frightened, but I had something very
important to ask him.

'Please, sir,' I said, my voice trembling, 'please may   20
I take this notice off my back before the boys come
back? — I am very sorry indeed, sir, that I behaved so
badly.'

Mr Creakle leapt up from his chair, and I ran. I did
not stop running until I reached my bedroom. I lay on   25
my bed trembling with fear for about two hours.

Luckily for me the first boy to return thought my
notice was very funny. His name was Tommy
Traddles. He introduced me to all the other boys
saying, 'Look at this! Here's a good game!'   30

Some boys pretended that I was a dog and stroked
me and said, 'Lie down, boy!' At first I did not like
this, but then I saw they were playing a game, and
being friendly. I decided that the notice was not as
bad for me as I had expected.   35

The oldest boy in the school was J. Steerforth. He was six years older than me. He was very kind to me. He helped me use my seven shillings to buy fruit, wine and cakes for the boys. We had a feast in our bedroom
5 in the middle of the night. The boys were pleased with the food, and at the feast they told me many things about the school.

Mr Mell loses control

Lessons began next day. The roar of voices in the
10 classroom suddenly stopped when Mr Creakle entered.
'Now, boys,' he whispered, 'this is a new term. Be careful to behave yourselves. I advise you to work hard at your lessons, for I shall work hard at the punishment if you don't. I won't hesitate. You won't be able to rub
15 out the marks I shall give you. Now, start working, all of you!'
When this dreadful speech was over, Mr Creakle came to my desk. He said that he knew I was famous for biting. He was famous for biting too, he said. He
20 showed me the stick. Wasn't that as sharp as a tooth? Couldn't it bite like a tooth? After each question he struck me with it, and very soon I was in tears.
Steerforth did his best to protect me and was a most useful friend. But he could not — or anyway he did not
25 — defend me from Mr Creakle, who was very cruel to me. There was one advantage in Mr Creakle's cruelty, however. He liked to strike me every time he walked past me, but he found my notice got in the way. For this reason it was soon taken off, and I did not see it
30 again.
I was helped a good deal by Mr Mell, who liked me, but I was unhappy to see that Steerforth treated him very badly.

One Saturday, poor Mr Mell was teaching and the noise in the room was terrible. There were laughing boys, singing boys, talking boys, dancing boys, shouting boys, running boys and joking boys everywhere.

'Silence!' cried Mr Mell, suddenly standing up. 'Why are you making so much noise? I have no more patience left. I am very annoyed with you. Do you realize how unfair you are being to me?'

The boys all stopped, some of them suddenly surprised, some half afraid, and perhaps some were sorry.

Steerforth was standing at the far end of the long room. He was leaning against the wall with his hands in his pockets, and looking at Mr Mell. Mr Mell thought he was whistling.

'Silence, Mr Steerforth,' said Mr Mell.

'Silence yourself,' said Steerforth, 'and don't give orders to me.'

'Sit down,' said Mr Mell.

'Sit down yourself,' said Steerforth.

Some of the boys laughed and a few clapped, but Mr Mell was so pale that they were immediately silent again.

'If you think, Steerforth, that you can use your power as a favourite here to be rude to a gentleman — '

'A gentleman! — I cannot see any gentlemen here!' said Steerforth.

Traddles cried out, 'Shame, J. Steerforth! That is too bad!'

Mr Mell told Traddles to be quiet, too. Then he continued, 'To be rude to someone whose life has been difficult and who has never harmed you is mean and dishonourable, Mr Steerforth. You can sit down or stand up as you like.'

'Wait a minute,' said Steerforth, coming to the front of the room. 'I tell you, Mr Mell, when you call me mean and dishonourable, you are a shameless beggar.'

Then, suddenly, the whole class was quiet and still. Mr Creakle had come in.

Mr Creakle was very angry. He said Mr Mell had lost control of the class. He said that he did not want Mr Mell to work at the school any longer, and told him to leave. Then he caned Tommy Traddles for crying because Mr Mell was leaving.

A few days after this, on my birthday, one of the teachers told me to go to Mr Creakle. I went happily, because I thought Peggotty had sent me a present, but when I saw both Mr and Mrs Creakle waiting for me in Mr Creakle's room, I knew something was wrong.

Mrs Creakle spoke to me in a sad voice. She said she had something to tell me about my mother. Then I knew. My poor mother was dead. I began to cry wildly. I did not know what to do. I felt that now I was completely alone in the world.

Mrs Creakle was very kind to me. She kept me with her all day. I cried until I was so tired that I fell asleep.

I left Salem House the next afternoon, and never returned.

3
I Start Work

Emily hears about Steerforth

After the funeral of my mother, the first thing that Miss Murdstone did was to dismiss Peggotty. She had to leave in a month's time. Peggotty said that she would stay with her brother at Yarmouth for two weeks. She asked Miss Murdstone if I could go with her. 5

'Oh!' said Miss Murdstone, 'My brother must not be troubled by such matters; he has too much to think about. I suppose the boy can go.'

At Yarmouth, Mr Peggotty and Ham were waiting for 10 us. We soon came within sight of Mr Peggotty's house; it looked just the same, and Mrs Gummidge was waiting at the door. But little Emily was not there. Mr Peggotty told me she was at school.

I knew which way Emily would come home, and 15 presently walked slowly along the path to meet her.

Then she came. She was prettier and gayer, and her blue eyes looked bluer than ever. I decided to play a game, and pretend I did not know her. I passed by looking into the distance, but little Emily did not care a 20 bit. She saw me plainly, and ran away, laughing. Of course I ran after her, and we were very near the cottage when I caught her.

'Oh, it's you, is it?' said little Emily.

'Oh, you knew who it was, Emily,' said I. 25

'And didn't you know who I was?' said Emily.

I was going to kiss her but she covered her red lips and said she was not a baby now.

She was so friendly and kind, and had such a pleasant manner that I liked her more than ever. 30

As we sat by the fire after tea I told them about Salem House, and particularly about Steerforth.

'He is very handsome,' said I, 'and such a generous, fine, noble young man that I cannot praise him enough.'

5 I was talking eagerly about Steerforth when I saw Emily's face; she was listening with full attention, her blue eyes shining like jewels, and her cheeks red. I stopped, surprised; and they all laughed and looked at her.

10 'Emily is like me,' said Peggotty, 'and would like to see young Mr Steerforth.'

Emily was ashamed and hid her face. Looking up a little later, and seeing that we were still all looking at her, she ran away. She did not come back until it was 15 nearly time to go to bed.

The time passed quickly and soon I had to return to my unfriendly home, but this time without Peggotty.

Responsible for my own life

After breakfast one morning, I was going out of the 20 room when Mr Murdstone told me to stay. A friend of his, Mr Quinion, was staying with us. He was standing with his hands in his pockets, looking out of the window.

'David,' said Mr Murdstone, 'young people should 25 not sit at home idle all the time. I am not rich, and education is expensive. I cannot keep you at school any longer. You will have to learn to be responsible for your own life, and you should begin as soon as possible.'

It seemed to me that I had already begun, in my 30 rather helpless way.

'You have heard me mention the business of Murdstone and Grinby in the wine trade. Mr Quinion here manages that business. There are a number of boys that have jobs there, and he suggests that you could be one of them. So you are now going to London, Davy, with Mr Quinion, to begin looking after yourself in the world.'

Murdstone and Grinby's

Murdstone and Grinby's was by the river. It was a strange old building, just at the edge of the water when the tide was in, and on the mud when the tide was out. I remember clearly its rotting floors and stairs, and the dirt, and the squeaking and scratching of old grey rats. The place was almost a ruin.

My job was to examine empty bottles by holding them up to the light; those with faults could not be used again. The others had to be washed. When there were no empty bottles to examine, there was always plenty of other work to be done. There were corks to be put in the full bottles, or finished bottles to be packed. This was my work and the work of two or three other boys.

All my hopes of growing up to be an educated and respectable gentleman were destroyed. I felt ashamed of my situation.

The Micawbers

At half past twelve on the first day, Mr Quinion knocked on the window of his office and signalled to me to go in, which I did. Inside was a rather fat, middle-aged person in a brown coat and black trousers and shoes. His large and shining head was as hairless as an egg, and his face was very large. His clothes were old and shapeless.

'This is Mr Micawber,' said Mr Quinion to me. 'Mr Murdstone knows Mr Micawber. He has written to him and Mr Micawber will let a room to you.'

Mr Quinion then officially gave me my job, at a salary of six shillings, which later rose to seven shillings, a week.

In the evening, at eight o'clock, Mr Micawber reappeared. I washed my hands and face and we walked to our house, as I suppose I should call it, together.

The house looked as poor as its owner, but also like its owner it was made to look as respectable as possible. Mr Micawber introduced me to Mrs Micawber, a thin and weak lady who was not young. She was holding a baby in her arms.

There were three other children, a boy aged about four, a girl aged about three and another baby.

Mrs Micawber came upstairs to show me the room. It was at the top of the house and had very little furniture in it. She sat down to rest after climbing the stairs.

'I never imagined before I was married that I would ever need to let rooms. But Mr Micawber is in difficulties, and so, you will understand, my own feelings must come second,' she said.

I said, 'Yes, Mrs Micawber.'

'If the people to whom Mr Micawber owes money will not give him time to pay, then they must accept the effect of their actions. Blood cannot be obtained from a stone, and neither can any money be obtained at present from Mr Micawber.'

The only visitors to that house that I ever saw or heard of, were men to whom Mr Micawber owed money. They used to come at all hours, and some of them were quite fierce.

In this house and with this family, I spent my free time. I provided my own breakfast — a little milk and a cheap loaf of bread — and my own supper — another small loaf and a little cheese.

The Micawbers were kind to me, but my life at that time was not happy. I worked from morning to night with rough men and boys, and was a poor and dirty child. I spent all the money I earned on my food and still did not eat properly. I wandered in the streets and I might even have become a thief, for no one looked after me or helped me. I kept my unhappiness a secret, and never let anyone know; I did not even tell Peggotty in the letters I wrote to her.

I considered my life to be hopeless, and did not expect to be saved from my loneliness or the shame of my job.

Mr Micawber goes to prison

Mr Micawber's problems made me even sadder. One evening Mrs Micawber talked to me privately.

'David Copperfield, I speak to you as a friend, and so I must tell you that Mr Micawber's difficulties have increased greatly,' she said. 'With the exception of a small piece of cheese, there is nothing to eat in the house.'

At last Mr Micawber owed so much money that he was arrested early one morning and taken to prison. The next Sunday I went to see him. He was waiting for me inside and we went up to his room. We cried a great deal. He advised me very seriously to take his life as a warning. Then he borrowed a shilling from me to buy some food.

Mr Micawber applied to be allowed out of prison under a special law. Mrs Micawber expected him to be free in about six weeks.

'And then,' said Mr Micawber, 'I have no doubt I shall have enough money, and live in a completely new way — if anything turns up.' He meant that he hoped he would have some good luck.

Finally, to my great joy, Mr Micawber was freed. I said to Mrs Micawber, 'May I ask, Mrs Micawber, what you and Mr Micawber intend to do, now that Mr Micawber is out of difficulties?'

'My family think Mr Micawber has great ability. They think that with a little influence he might find a job in the government,' said Mrs Micawber. She always said 'my family' in a way that made them sound like very important people.

'My family think Mr Micawber should go down to Plymouth, to be ready and in the right place, in case anything turns up there.'

'And will you go too, Mrs Micawber?'

Mrs Micawber cried as she replied:

'I will never leave Mr Micawber. Although Mr Micawber hid his difficulties from me at first, I will never leave Mr Micawber. No!' cried Mrs Micawber, 'I never will!'

The Micawbers go to Plymouth

I thought about leaving the Micawbers, and being forced to live once more with new people. I realized that without the friendship of the Micawbers my present life was lonely and hopeless. I knew that my situation would not change unless I planned an escape myself.

When the Micawbers had to leave we all felt sad about our separation.

'I shall never, David Copperfield, remember the time when Mr Micawber was in difficulties without thinking of you,' said Mrs Micawber. 'You have been a great friend.'

I said I was very sorry they were going away.

'My dear young friend,' said Mr Micawber, 'I am a man with some experience of life. Until something turns up (which I am sure it will very soon), I can only give you some advice, but my advice is valuable. If I had listened to it I would not have been in difficulties. My advice is, never leave until tomorrow the things you can do today. My other piece of advice, Copperfield, is this: salary twenty pounds, expenses nineteen pounds, result — happiness; salary twenty pounds, expenses twenty-one pounds, result — ruin.'

Next morning I met the whole family and saw them sadly get into the back of the carriage.

'David Copperfield,' said Mrs Micawber, 'good luck! I shall never forget all you have done for us.'

'Copperfield,' said Mr Micawber, 'goodbye! I wish you wealth and happiness. If something turns up (I am rather certain it will), I shall be very happy to help you.'

The carriage started, and I could hardly see the family because they waved so many handkerchieves. In a minute they had gone. I went away to begin my tiring day at Murdstone and Grinby's.

However, I did not intend to work many more days there. I had decided to run away. I had decided to go, somehow, to the only relative I had in the whole world. I would go to my aunt, Miss Betsy Trotwood, and tell her my troubles. Peggotty had told me that Miss Trotwood owned a small cottage somewhere near Dover.

I waited until Saturday night, and then I ran away as I had planned.

4

Betsy Trotwood

I find my way to Dover

Perhaps I thought I could run all the way to Dover. In fact I had to stop and rest just outside London. I was very tired with the effort I had already made. It was ten o'clock, and a dark but warm night. The weather was fine.

I had planned to spend the night behind the wall at the back of my old school. I imagined I would not feel so lonely; it would give me some comfort to be so near the boys, even if they did not know I was there.

With some trouble I found Salem House, and the particular place where I had decided to sleep. I lay down. I shall never forget the lonely feeling of lying down for the first time without a roof over my head.

The warm sun and the ringing of the morning bell at Salem House woke me up. I crept away from the wall as Mr Creakle's boys were getting up, and found the road that led to Dover. I walked, that Sunday, twenty-three long miles. At last I crept onto a bank of grass at the side of a lane. Here I lay down, and soon fell asleep.

When I set off again the next morning, I found myself walking between fields of trees with ripe red apples on them. I thought the countryside was very beautiful, and I decided to sleep under the trees that night.

I managed to walk another twenty miles along that road. My legs felt stiff and weak, and my feet were sore when at last I lay down to sleep among the trees. Next day I reached the wide open hills beside the sea near Dover. I arrived at Dover itself after six days' walking.

I asked some boatmen about my aunt first, but got no information. No one answered my questions seriously. The shopkeepers were all sure I must be a beggar, and sent me away before I could ask them anything. I felt more unhappy and lonely than at any time on the journey from London. I was hungry, thirsty and weak, but they still joked and made up stories.

I was sitting on the step of an empty shop when I saw a driver who looked kind. I decided to ask him.

'Trotwood,' said he, 'I know that name. Is she an old lady?'

'Yes,' I said, 'rather old.'

'Go up there and walk until you see some houses facing the sea,' he said, pointing towards a hill.

After walking quite a long way I saw the houses. I went into a little shop nearby, and asked them if they could tell me where Miss Trotwood lived. I had spoken to the shopkeeper, who was weighing some rice for a young woman. But the young woman turned round quickly, as if I had spoken to her, and said, 'Miss Trotwood? Why do you want to see her, boy?' She told me that she was my aunt's servant.

'I want to speak to her, please Miss,' I said.

The young woman put her rice in a little basket and walked out of the shop. She told me I could follow her if I wanted to know where Miss Trotwood lived. We soon came to a very neat little cottage. In front was a small, square garden, full of flowers.

'This is Miss Trotwood's house,' said the servant. 'Now you know.' Then she hurried inside to show that she was not responsible for my arrival.

David meets his aunt

A lady came out of the house. I knew immediately that

she was Miss Betsy. She looked exactly like the woman my mother so often described to me.

'Go away!' said Miss Betsy, shaking her head. 'Go away! We don't want any boys here!' I was not surprised my aunt did not want to look at me. My clothes were in a terrible condition. They were torn, shapeless and dirty. My hair had not been combed for many days, and I was covered from head to foot with dust from the road.

I had no courage, but my need was great. I went into the garden softly, and stood beside her, and touched her with my finger.

'Please, Miss Trotwood,' I began.

She stood and looked at me.

'Please, Aunt, I am your nephew.'

'Goodness!' said my aunt, and sat down suddenly on the garden path.

'I am David Copperfield, of Blunderstone, — '

I tried to explain why I had come; but suddenly I could not control myself any longer. I burst into tears. My aunt got up in a great hurry and took me into the sitting room. Here the first thing she did was to ring the bell.

'Janet,' said my aunt when her servant came in, 'go upstairs and heat some water for the bath!'

Janet looked a little surprised, but she went. My aunt walked up and down the room. She was a tall lady, with a rather fierce face and manner. But her appearance was certainly not unpleasant. She had bright eyes and grey hair.

The room was as neat as my aunt. The solid furniture was brightly rubbed and polished. I saw a cat, two tame birds, a bowl full of dried rose leaves, and a tall cupboard. Behind the glass doors of this cupboard were all kinds of bottles and pots.

When I had had a bath, my aunt and Janet gave me a clean shirt and a pair of trousers which they had borrowed from a neighbour. Feeling very faint and tired, I soon fell asleep in a chair.

When I woke up I thought I had been dreaming. I imagined my aunt had come and bent over me, and had brushed my hair away from my face. I thought I had heard the words 'pretty boy' and 'poor lad'.

We had dinner soon after I woke up. Not until after this did my aunt ask me about my life. Gradually, after a number of questions, she discovered all that had happened. When I started to tell her about my mother's death, and about Peggotty, I burst into tears and could not speak. I hid my face in my hands on the table.

'If the bed is ready,' said my aunt to Janet, 'we'll take him up to it.'

When I went downstairs in the morning, my aunt was sitting at the breakfast table. She was looking very serious. She said that she had written to Mr Murdstone to tell him what had happened. I was very frightened, and asked my aunt if I would have to go back to live with him.

'I don't know,' said Miss Betsy. 'We shall see.'

A week later, Mr and Miss Murdstone came to my aunt's cottage. They told my aunt many bad things about me. They said that I had a terrible temper, that I was ungrateful for what they had done for me, and that I had behaved like a beggar. They had come to take me back with them. If I was not willing to go, they said, they would never let me into their house again.

Then my aunt told Mr Murdstone that she did not believe any of the things they had said about me. She said she would make a home for me with her. Without saying any more, Mr and Miss Murdstone both walked
5 out of the cottage.

At Mr Wickfield's

My aunt and I were soon good friends, and the time passed very pleasantly.

'David,' she said one evening, 'we must consider
10 your education. Would you like to go to school at Canterbury?'

I replied that I would like it very much. Canterbury was not far from Dover, so I would still be near to her.

We went to Canterbury the following day. First we
15 stopped at the office of my aunt's lawyer, Mr Wickfield. My aunt asked him to suggest a school where I would be well taught and well treated. After some discussion he took my aunt to see a school he thought would be suitable. I waited for them in Mr
20 Wickfield's office.

While I was waiting I could see into another, smaller office. A thin young man with red hair was working there. I thought he could not see me, but later I realized that he could. I began to feel very uncomfortable. Every
25 few minutes he secretly stared at me for a minute at a time. Meanwhile his pen went on writing, or pretended to.

At last my aunt and Mr Wickfield came back. My aunt had liked the school. They had decided that I
30 should go there as a day student, and that I would live with Mr Wickfield.

'Come with me and meet my little servant,' Mr Wickfield said to us.

We went upstairs and into a shady old room. The windows of this room all had wooden seats under them. It was full of strange little corners, each with a small table or bookcase or seat in it. Mr Wickfield knocked quietly on a door and a girl of about my own age came out quickly and kissed him. Although her face was quite bright and happy, she had a peaceful calm manner that I have never forgotten, and never will forget.

'This is my little servant, my daughter Agnes,' Mr Wickfield said. I heard how he said this, and saw him hold her hand, and I guessed that she was the one joy of his life.

My aunt told me that everything would be arranged for me by Mr Wickfield. Then she spoke to me very kindly and gave me some valuable advice.

She said, 'David, do as well as I know you can, for your own sake and mine. Never be mean over anything. Never be dishonest. Never be cruel. If you avoid these three things I think you will do well.'

I promised I would remember her advice. Then she kissed me quickly and went out.

At five o'clock Mr Wickfield usually ate dinner. The table was only laid for us two, but Agnes sat opposite her father. I do not think he would have eaten if she had not been there.

After dinner I wandered downstairs. I saw the young man with red hair shutting the office door. Feeling friendly towards everybody, I went in and spoke to him. He told me his name was Uriah Heep. When I left we shook hands, but oh, what a cold wet hand he had! It felt as strange as it looked. I rubbed mine to warm it, and to rub his off! It was such an unpleasant hand that when I went to my room afterwards I could still remember the cold, wet feel of it clearly.

5

The Humble Mr Heep

At Canterbury

Next morning, after breakfast, I started school again. I was introduced by Mr Wickfield to Dr Strong, who was the owner and the headmaster.

5   Dr Strong took me to the classroom, which was a large hall on the quietest side of the house. About twenty-five boys were working when we went in. They stood up to say good morning to Dr Strong, and remained standing when they saw Mr Wickfield and

10   me.

'A new boy: David Copperfield,' said Dr Strong.

The oldest boy then stepped out of his place and welcomed me. He showed me my desk and introduced me to the masters.

15   I felt strange because I had not lived with boys for so long. While I was at Murdstone and Grinby's I had never played sports and games. Now I had forgotten how. When I was examined I knew nothing, and was put in the lowest class in the school.

20   I went back to Mr Wickfield's house after school was over. There was such a friendly feeling there that my worries disappeared. Agnes was in the sitting room with her father. She met me, smiling pleasantly, and asked me whether I liked the school. I said I expected I

25   would like it very much, but that it was rather strange at first. Mr Wickfield told me I would be happy with Dr Strong, who was one of the kindest men he knew.

After dinner we went up to the sitting room again. Agnes worked, and talked to Mr Wickfield. She played

30   some games with me, and looked at my schoolbooks. After she had gone to bed, Mr Wickfield said to me,

'Would you like to stay with us, David, or go somewhere else?'

'I would like to stay here,' I answered quickly.

'You are a fine lad, a friend for both Agnes and me. As long as you enjoy being here you may stay.'

He told me that I could come down to his room at any time in the evening, to sit with him or to read. I thanked him for his thoughtfulness.

I was going downstairs later, when I saw a light in the little office. I felt a kind of interest in Uriah Heep, and I immediately went in. Uriah was reading a big fat book, with great attention. His thin finger followed every line as he read.

David talks with Uriah Heep

'You are working late tonight, Uriah,' I said.

'Yes, Mr Copperfield,' said Uriah.

I noticed that he could not smile like other people did; he could only make his mouth wider to look like a smile.

'I am improving my knowledge of the law, Mr Copperfield,' said Uriah.

'I suppose you are quite a great lawyer?' I said.

'Me, Mr Copperfield?' said Uriah. 'Oh no! I'm a very humble person, Mr Copperfield, I'm very poor and unimportant.'

I had not just imagined that Uriah had wet hands. He was continually rubbing them together as if he were trying to make them dry and warm. Often he wiped them secretly on his handkerchief.

'I know I am a humble person,' said Uriah. 'My mother is poor and unimportant, too, so she is a humble person, like me. And we live in a humble house, Mr Copperfield, but we have a great deal to be thankful for.'

I asked Uriah if he had worked for Mr Wickfield for long.

'I have worked for him for nearly four years, Mr Copperfield,' said Uriah. 'Since the year after my father's death. I am so thankful for Mr Wickfield's kindness to me!'

'Perhaps you will be a partner in Mr Wickfield's business, and it will be called "Wickfield and Heep".'

'Oh, no, Mr Copperfield,' replied Uriah. 'I am much too humble for that! Mr Wickfield is an excellent man, Mr Copperfield. And your aunt is a sweet lady, Mr Copperfield!'

He had a way of twisting himself about like a snake when he spoke. This was very ugly. I could not listen to what he was saying because I was watching his body twisting.

'A sweet lady, Mr Copperfield!' said Uriah Heep. 'She greatly admires Miss Agnes, doesn't she, Mr Copperfield?'

'I am sure everybody does,' I replied.

'Oh, thank you, Mr Copperfield, for that remark,' he said. 'It is so true! Though I am humble, I know it is so true! Oh, thank you, Mr Copperfield!'

He became so excited that he nearly twisted himself off his stool. 'Mother will be expecting me at home, soon,' he said. 'Although we are very humble people, Mr Copperfield, we are very fond of each other. Perhaps you would like to come one afternoon and have a cup of tea at our poor home. Mother would be as proud as I would be.'

I said I would be glad to come.

At last he was ready to leave the office for the night. He put out the light, and shook hands with me. His hand felt like a fish in the dark. Uriah then opened the door into the street a little way, and crept out.

A visit to the Heeps

I gradually felt happier at school among my new companions. I began to work very hard. Soon my life at Murdstone and Grinby's seemed almost like a bad dream; I began to feel as though I had been at Dr 5 Strong's school for a long time. It was an excellent school. It was as different from Mr Creakle's school as right is from wrong. Everyone in the town thought well of the schoolboys, and we never did anything to make Dr Strong ashamed of us. Some of the older boys lived 10 in his house. From them I discovered that Dr Strong was worshipped by the whole school. He was one of the kindest men in the world.

One Thursday morning when I was setting off for school, I met Uriah in the street. He reminded me of the 15 promise I had made to have tea with him and his mother.

'But you do not need to keep your promise, Mr Copperfield. I am sure we are too humble for you to want to visit us.' 20

I had not really been able to decide whether I liked Uriah or not. However, I did not want him to think I was proud. I said I was only waiting to be invited.

'Oh, if it is not because we are so humble, then that's all right, Mr Copperfield. Will you come this evening?' 25 said Uriah.

I said I would mention it to Mr Wickfield and if he agreed I would come with pleasure. So, at six o'clock that evening I told Uriah I was ready.

'Mother will be so proud,' he said as we walked 30 away from the office together. 'Or she would be proud, if being proud were not wicked, Mr Copperfield.'

'Have you been studying much law, recently?' I asked.

'Oh, Mr Copperfield, my reading can't be called study. I just read law books for an hour or two in the evening sometimes.'

We came to a small house. The door was open. We walked into a low room and there we met Mrs Heep. She was exactly like Uriah, but short.

'We will always remember this day, Uriah, when Mr Copperfield visited us,' said Mrs Heep, as she was making the tea.

'I said you would be proud, mother,' said Uriah.

'I wish Mr Heep were still alive,' said Mrs Heep. 'I know he would have liked to meet Mr Copperfield.'

I felt uncomfortable when they said these things, but I knew I was being treated as an honoured guest.

'My Uriah has looked forward to this for a long time, sir,' said Mrs Heep. 'He was afraid you would not come because we are too humble, and I was afraid of it too. But humble we are, humble we have been, and humble we shall ever be,' said Mrs Heep.

We sat at a small table. Mrs Heep gradually moved nearer to me, and Uriah gradually moved opposite me. They respectfully offered me all the nicest food.

Presently they began to talk about aunts, and I told them about mine. They talked about mothers, and I told them about mine. Then Mrs Heep began to talk about fathers. I began to tell her about mine, but stopped because my aunt had advised me to keep silent on that matter.

I had no chance against Uriah and Mrs Heep. They persuaded me to talk about matters I had no wish to talk about. They worked together to find out all they could about me.

When they had enough interesting information about me they started to discuss Mr Wickfield and Agnes. They talked so much, and about so many things, that I could not understand the conversation at all. First they discussed the excellence of Mr Wickfield. Then they discussed how much I admired Agnes. After that they wondered how large Mr Wickfield's business was, and how rich he was. All the time I found myself telling them things that I should not tell them.

Mr Micawber again

I was beginning to wish I could escape from the visit. Suddenly a person walking down the street passed the open door, came back again, and cried out loudly, 'Copperfield!' It was Mr Micawber!

I was glad to see him, and shook hands eagerly. I could not avoid introducing Mr Micawber to Uriah Heep and his mother, but I was anxious to leave, and soon afterwards we walked out together.

Mr Micawber took me to his hotel. Here, lying on a small bed, was Mrs Micawber.

Mrs Micawber told me that Mr Micawber had not been able to find work in Plymouth. His relatives thought he should become a trader, but he did not have enough money. They had come to Canterbury in the hope that something would turn up there.

I had dinner with them a few days later. I was surprised to hear that Mr Micawber and Uriah Heep
5 had become friends.

'And I can tell you, my dear Copperfield, that young man, Heep, might be a very important lawyer one day,' said Mr Micawber. 'If I had known him when my difficulties were greatest, I would have managed a lot
10 better.'

I could not understand this remark, but I did not like to ask what he meant.

We had a very enjoyable dinner. They did not mention leaving Canterbury. I was therefore very
15 surprised to hear the next day that the whole family had gone to London.

6
Old Friends

Changes

I do not remember feeling sorry when I finished school, three years later. To me, at that time, life was like a great fairy story, and I was just beginning to enjoy reading it.

My aunt and I had many discussions about my future. For more than a year I had tried to find a satisfactory answer to her question; 'What would you like to do?' But though she asked me many times, there was nothing I particularly wanted to do. One cold morning, soon after I had left school, my aunt said to me, 'David, I think a little change would help you to decide what you want to do. You should live in the country for a while. Would you like to go and see that strange woman with the silly name?' She meant Peggotty.

'I would like to do that more than anything else!'

'Oh,' said my aunt, 'that's lucky, for I should like it too. I shall send you on your journey alone, so you will have to look after yourself and begin to make your own decisions.'

When we separated, my aunt gave me some good advice and a lot of kisses. She suggested that I should stay in London for a few days, either on my way to Suffolk, or on my way back. In fact, I was given permission to do what I liked for three weeks or a month.

I went to Canterbury first, to say goodbye to Agnes and Mr Wickfield. Agnes was very glad to see me. She told me the house had been different since I had left. Then, looking worried, she said, 'David, there is something I want to ask you, and this may be my last chance for a long time. Have you noticed a change in Father?'

I had noticed a change. Agnes saw from my face that I understood what she meant. She looked down immediately, and I could see that she had tears in her eyes.

'Tell me how he has changed,' she said.

'I do not think he is well, and he is often worried. His hand trembles, his speech is not clear and his eyes look wild. I have also noticed that at these times he is often called away to deal with some business,' I said.

'By Uriah,' Agnes said.

'Yes,' I replied.

Soon I left for London. I compared this journey with my journey down from London to Dover. Now I was well educated, well dressed, and I had plenty of money in my pocket. I looked out for the places where I had slept on my long walk. At last we passed Salem House, a few miles outside London. I wanted to stop and cane Mr Creakle, and let all the boys out of the school. They seemed like birds locked in a cage.

David meets Steerforth and Rosa Dartle

I stayed in a hotel in London. After dinner I sat for some time by the fire, and then I got up to go to bed. As I was going I passed someone whose face seemed familiar. I turned, came back, and looked again. He did not know me, but I knew him at once. It was Steerforth.

We were very pleased to see each other. We spent the rest of the evening telling each other about our lives since we had last seen each other at Salem House. Then Steerforth invited me to stay for a day or two at his home. I accepted the invitation happily.

When we arrived, Steerforth introduced me to his mother and another lady who was introduced as Miss Dartle. Both Steerforth and his mother called her Rosa. I discovered that she lived there. She had been Mrs Steerforth's companion for a long time.

Rosa Dartle was small and dark, and did not look very pleasant. I was curious about her. Perhaps this was because of something really unusual about her. She had a mark on her lip from an old wound which had healed years ago. I was told later that this wound had been caused by Steerforth. He had cut her with a knife when they were both children, and she had never forgiven him. I could hardly see it now, across the table. But on and above her upper lip it still showed. I decided secretly that she was about thirty years old, and that she would like to be married.

Mrs Steerforth spoke to me about my plan to go to Suffolk. I said I would be glad if Steerforth would go with me. I told them about the Peggottys and their boat-house. Steerforth said he thought it would be worth a journey to see people like that.

Little Emily

We said goodbye to Mrs Steerforth and Miss Dartle and went to Yarmouth together.

'When do you intend to introduce me to the Peggottys?' said Steerforth. It was the following morning, and we were having a late breakfast at our hotel.

'I thought this evening would be a good time. They will all be sitting round the fire. I shall not give them any warning that we are here,' said I. 'We must surprise them.'

5   'Of course! It's no fun unless we surprise them,' said Steerforth. 'You are hoping to see your nurse, I suppose?'

'Oh yes,' I said. 'I want to see Peggotty most of all.'

At eight o'clock that evening we set out for Mr
10 Peggotty's, walking together over the dark cold sand towards the old boat.

'This is a wild kind of place, Steerforth, isn't it?'

'It seems quite dangerous in the dark,' he said. 'And the sea roars like a hungry animal that wants to swallow
15 us up. Is that the boat? I can see a light over there.'

'That's the boat,' said I.

We said no more. We walked towards the light and went quietly to the door. I put my hand on it, and whispered to Steerforth to keep close to me. I went in.

20   I found myself in the middle of the family. They were so surprised they just stared at me. I held my hand out to Mr Peggotty. Then Ham shouted:

'Young Davy! It's young Master Davy!'

Immediately we were all shaking hands with each
25 other. Mr Peggotty was so proud and delighted to see us that he did not know what to do. I shook hands again and again, and laughed joyfully.

Then Peggotty came in. At first she did not recognize me. Then she stepped back and put out her hands as if
30 she were frightened and wanted to keep me away.

'Peggotty!' I cried to her.

'My dear boy!' she said. She held me in her arms, and we both cried.

I had never cried and laughed so much as I did that
35 evening. I then introduced them all to Steerforth. I had

told them a great deal about him on my last visit. Mr
Peggotty immediately cried, 'Emily, my darling, come
here! Come here, my little girl! Here's the gentleman
you have heard about, Emily. He has come with Davy to
see you. This is our little Emily, sir,' he continued in a   5
low voice to Steerforth. 'No one could make a house as
cheerful and happy as Emily has made this one. She
isn't my child. I never had one. But I love her as much
as I could love any child. You understand! I couldn't
love my own child more!'   10

'I do understand,' said Steerforth.

'I know you do, sir,' replied Mr Peggotty. 'And thank
you. But no one can know how important little Emily is
to me.'

Mr Peggotty's news   15

Mr Peggotty brushed his untidy hair back with his
hand. Then he went on speaking, with a hand on each
of his knees:

'There is a person who has known our little Emily
from the time when her father was drowned. He is a   20
handsome person; he is rather like me to look at —
rough, because he works out of doors — but an honest
sort of man, and a kind one.' I thought I had never seen
Ham smile as much as he was smiling now.

'And what did he do? He decided he loved our little Emily,' said Mr Peggotty. Mr Peggotty laid a hand on my knee, and the other on Steerforth's. Then he said to us, 'Suddenly one evening little Emily left her work and came in with him. And this person took hold of her hand, and said to me, joyfully, "Look! She is going to be my little wife!" And, half bold, and half frightened, and half laughing, she said, "Yes, Uncle, please."'

Ham, with great difficulty, said, 'She is very precious to me — gentlemen. She's all I can ever want, and more — more than I can say. I — I love her truly.'

I could not help feeling sad about little Emily and Ham, but in a few minutes we were all very happy again.

It was almost midnight when we left. We separated merrily. They all stood in a crowd round the door. I saw little Emily's dear blue eyes looking as we went, and I heard her soft voice calling to us to be careful.

'She is a beautiful young girl!' said Steerforth, putting his arm through mine.

'How lucky we are to have come now, to hear about their happiness and intended marriage. I have never seen people so happy. But he is rather a dull, stupid young man for the girl, isn't he?' said Steerforth.

He had been very cheerful with Ham, and with them all, so I was shocked to hear this unfriendly remark.

But the next minute he was happily singing a song that Mr Peggotty had taught him, and we walked quickly back to our hotel.

Steerforth and I stayed for more than two weeks in that part of the country. Then, while we were eating breakfast one morning, I was given a letter. It was from my aunt. She had gone to stay for a week in London to arrange my future work and wanted to meet me there. We decided to say goodbye to the Peggottys, and go back to London that day. When our journey ended, Steerforth went home. I went to my aunt's hotel where I found her waiting for me.

Work, and a home in London

My aunt had decided that I should work as a lawyer. She asked me what I thought about her plan.

'I like it very much,' I said.

The next day, we set off for the office of Spenlow and Jorkins, lawyers. The office was down a quiet street, away from the noise of the city. I was introduced by my aunt to Mr Spenlow, and it was soon settled that I should begin. I would try the work for one month, and if I liked it I could then stay, and study to be a lawyer.

We left the office, and then talked about where I should live. My aunt had seen a newspaper advertisement for some rooms to let with a view of the river, so we went to look at them. The rooms were on the top floor of the house and the river was outside the window, just as the advertisement had said. I was delighted with the place. My aunt talked to the landlady about how much I should pay, and the next day I moved into my new home.

7

The New Partner

A letter from Agnes

It was wonderful to have those rooms to myself. After two days and nights I felt as though I had lived there for a year.

Early on the third day I walked over to see Mrs Steerforth. She was very glad to see me, and said that James had gone for a holiday with one of his friends from the university. Miss Dartle was very interested to hear about all the things we had done at Yarmouth.

The next morning I received a letter from Agnes Wickfield. It just said, 'My dear David. I am staying at the house of Father's friend, Mr Waterbrook, in Ely Place, Holborn. Will you come and see me while I am here, any time you like? Yours sincerely, Agnes.'

I left the office at half past three. Half an hour later I reached Mr Waterbrook's house. A servant led me into a small sitting room, and there I saw Agnes sewing.

'Sit down,' said Agnes cheerfully. Then she asked me if I had seen Uriah.

'Uriah Heep?' I asked. 'No. Is he in London?'

'He comes to the office downstairs, every day,' replied Agnes. 'I think he is going to become a partner in the business with Father.'

'What? Uriah? How has that "humble" man managed to get such a position?' I cried. 'You must not allow your father to do this. You must stop him, Agnes, while you can!'

She replied, after a short silence, 'Uriah has been very useful to Father. He is skilful and watches everything. He has taken advantage of Father's weaknesses, and now Father is afraid of him.'

She might have said more. She suspected worse things. I clearly saw this, and remained silent.

'His power over Father is very great,' said Agnes. 'He says he is unimportant, but I fear he uses his power as often as possible.'

I said he was a dog, and I enjoyed saying it.

'Father has been very worried,' cried Agnes. 'But he seemed to be relieved to have Uriah as his partner. At the same time he seemed to be ashamed of it.'

'And what did you think, Agnes?'

'I did what I thought was right, David,' she replied. 'I thought that Father's peace was most important. For this, the sacrifice is not too great. So I encouraged him to do it. I said it would be a relief to him and make him less anxious. Oh David!' she cried, 'I almost feel that I have been his enemy, instead of his dear child.'

I had never seen Agnes cry before. I had never seen her sad. It made me so sorry that I could only say, foolishly, 'Please Agnes, don't cry! Don't, my dear sister!'

Her sadness passed, and her calm manner came back again.

'While I have the opportunity, David, let me speak to you. Be friendly to Uriah. Don't refuse to talk to him. Think instead of Father and me.'

Agnes had not time to say any more. Mrs Waterbrook, who was a large lady, came in. In fact she seemed to sail in, like a boat. She said she had heard Agnes speak kindly of me. She invited me to have dinner there the next day. I accepted the invitation, and said goodbye.

Mr Wickfield's foolishness

I went to dinner at Ely Place next day, and found Uriah Heep there. He was wearing a black suit.

There were other guests. I looked with particular
5 interest when one of them came in. He was introduced as Mr Traddles!

I turned to Mr Waterbrook, and told him that Mr Traddles was an old friend of mine. He replied that Traddles was now studying law, and did some work for
10 him sometimes.

Later, I was glad to be able to speak to Agnes. I introduced Traddles to her.

Traddles had to leave early, because he was going away next morning for a month. However, we
15 exchanged addresses, and promised to meet again when he returned. We both looked forward to this with pleasure. Traddles was very interested to hear that I knew Steerforth and seemed to like him very much.

I stayed, talking to Agnes and listening to her sing. I
20 did not want to be friendly to Uriah, but I remembered the request Agnes had made to me. When everyone else had gone, I went to speak to him.

'You have heard something, I suppose, about my new position, Mr Copperfield?' Uriah said.
25 'Yes,' I said, 'Miss Wickfield told me a little.'

'I'm so glad to find Miss Agnes knows about it. Oh, what a good man Mr Wickfield is, Mr Copperfield! But how foolish he has been!'

'Mr Wickfield is worth so much more than you or
30 me, and yet you say he has been foolish, Mr Heep,' I said.

'Oh, very foolish indeed, Mr Copperfield,' replied Uriah, sighing. 'Yes, really. Oh, anyone else would have completely ruined Mr Wickfield. There would have been loss, shame and more too, Mr Wickfield knows that. But I have always served him obediently. And now he has given me a position I could hardly hope to have. I should be so thankful!'

Uriah's wicked plan

I remember how frightened I was then. I could see from his face that he was preparing to say something else.

'You thought Miss Agnes looked very beautiful tonight, didn't you, Mr Copperfield?'

'I thought she looked better in every way than everyone round her. She always does,' I replied.

'Oh, thank you, thank you, Mr Copperfield! It's true!' he cried. 'Humble as I am and humble as my mother is, I have loved Miss Agnes secretly for years. I don't mind trusting you with my secret, Mr Copperfield. Oh, Mr Copperfield, I love the ground Miss Agnes walks on.'

I believe I had a wild idea of striking him over the head. But I looked at him and remembered Agnes's prayer. I kept as calm as I could. I asked him whether Agnes knew about his feelings.

'Oh no, Mr Copperfield,' he replied. 'Oh no! I hope she will see how useful I am to her father. I hope she will see how I manage his business for him. She is so fond of him. I think she may then be kind to me.'

I then understood the whole wicked plan. I also understood why he had explained it to me.

'There is no need to hurry, at present, you know, Mr Copperfield,' Uriah continued in his slippery manner. 'My Agnes is very young still. I have plenty of time to let her know how I feel. Oh, I am so grateful to you for this little talk!'

He took my hand to say goodbye, and gave it a squeeze. His own still felt unpleasantly cold and wet.

I did not see Uriah Heep again until the day when Agnes left London. I went to say goodbye to her and Uriah was there too. He was travelling to Canterbury at the same time.

Dora

One day, when I was working at Spenlow and Jorkins, Mr Spenlow told me his daughter was coming home from Paris soon. She had been finishing her education there. He said he would be very pleased if I would come to stay at his house the following Saturday.

When Mr Spenlow introduced me to Dora I found myself looking at a very beautiful young woman. At that moment I knew that I loved Dora Spenlow wildly. I did not pause or consider the situation. I had not spoken one word to her, but I knew I was her slave.

Then, to my great surprise, I heard someone say, 'I have seen Mr Copperfield before.' It was a voice that I remembered very well. It was Miss Murdstone!

'Mr Copperfield and I once knew each other,' said Miss Murdstone. 'That was when he was a child.'

'My daughter, unhappily, has no mother,' said Mr Spenlow to me. 'Miss Murdstone kindly acts as her companion and guide.' 5

But I could only look at Dora. I do not remember who was at dinner, except Dora. I have no idea what we had for dinner, besides Dora. I sat next to her. I talked to her. She had the most delightful little voice and the gayest little laugh and the most wonderful little 10 manner. She was rather small. That made her even more beautiful, I thought.

I do not remember much about the rest of the evening. I remember that Dora sang, and that she smiled at me once and that I went to bed feeling very weak. 15

Visitors

Traddles lived in a rather poor part of London. When I went there to see him I found that he was staying with my old friends, the Micawbers. We were very surprised to see each other again. I asked Traddles and the 20 Micawbers to visit me. One evening they came and we had a good meal and a happy time together.

After they had left I sat quietly in my room, by the fire, and thought about my life. My thoughts were half cheerful, half sad. Traddles was studying hard to be a 25 lawyer, but he was very poor. The Micawbers were still in difficulties, but, as usual, they were sure something good would turn up very soon. And then I began to think about my old nurse and her family at Yarmouth.

As I was thinking about them all I suddenly heard 30 quick steps on the stairs. It was Steerforth.

'Oh, David!' laughed Steerforth, shaking my hand eagerly. 'I have just come from Yarmouth.'

'Did you stay long there?'

'No, only a week or two.'

'Listen, Steerforth. I was just thinking I might go to Yarmouth to see my old nurse again. She will be so 5 pleased. And she will find it a comfort to see me. The journey is not too far to visit Peggotty, who has done so much for me. I'm sure you agree, don't you?'

Steerforth sat and considered my question and then answered in a low voice, 'Well, go if you wish. It cannot 10 do any harm. I am going to my mother's house tonight. Were you planning to go to Yarmouth tomorrow?'

'Yes, I think so.'

'Don't go for a few days, David. Come home with me, and stay as long as you can with us. Come. We may 15 never meet again.'

I thanked him very much, and he put on his coat and set off to walk home.

8
Emily Leaves Home

David says goodbye to Steerforth

I mentioned to Mr Spenlow that I wanted to go away for a short time. As I was not being paid, it was not difficult to arrange this.

Mrs Steerforth was pleased to see me, and so was Rosa Dartle, though I did not know why. Miss Dartle watched me particularly carefully. I noticed this when I had only been in the house for about an hour.

We all four went out for a walk in the afternoon. Rosa Dartle seized my arm with her thin hand and held me back. When Steerforth and his mother had walked on, and could not hear, she turned and looked straight at me. I saw the mark of the old wound stretch until it reached the lip which had been cut very badly. This mark and her bright eyes as she looked at me almost frightened me. She said, 'What is he doing?'

She said this with an eagerness that seemed to burn like fire in her.

'Is he angry, or proud, or in love? What is he feeling?'

'Miss Dartle,' I replied, 'I do not know of any way in which Steerforth has changed since I first came here. I hardly understand what you mean.'

'You must never tell anyone about this conversation!' she said in a quick, fierce way. She said no more.

There was something else about Miss Dartle I must not forget to mention. Steerforth had made an effort to please her, and be a pleasant companion. It needed great skill to do this. I saw her try, more and more weakly, to refuse his friendship. At first she seemed angry that he had so much power over her. Then I saw her smile gently as we sat by the fire. We talked and laughed together as if we were children.

'Don't get up,' said Steerforth. She had at last decided to go to bed. 'My dear Rosa, don't get up. Be
5 kind for once and sing us a song. Let me sit and listen as I used to do.'

She sang wildly and with great feeling. Her low voice and the music seemed to express all she felt and thought. I imagined I was dreaming. A minute later
10 Steerforth went over to her and put his arm round her shoulders. He was laughing as he said, 'See, Rosa, we still love each other very much.' Suddenly she hit him, and pushed him away from her in great anger, like a wild beast. She rushed out of the room.

15 'What is the matter with Rosa?' said Mrs Steerforth, coming in.

'She has been good and sweet, Mother, for a little while, so now she must be the opposite,' replied Steerforth.

20 Rosa did not come back. Steerforth laughed about what had happened. He asked me if I had ever seen anyone so strange and fierce.

I told him I was surprised at her behaviour. I asked if he could guess what had suddenly made her so
25 unhappy.

'Oh, I don't know at all,' said he. 'She watches everything and everyone. She's dangerous. Goodnight!'

'Goodnight, my dear Steerforth!' said I. 'I shall have to leave before you wake up in the morning.
30 Goodnight.'

He was unwilling to let me go.

'David, if for any reason we should be separated, think of me kindly.'

'I always do, Steerforth,' said I. 'I always love you
35 and treasure you.'

'Goodnight, David, and goodbye!'

We shook hands and we separated. I looked into his room in the morning, but he was asleep. He slept with his head on his arm, as I had often seen him sleep at school. And thus, in the silence of the early morning, I left him.

A light for Emily

I arrived in Yarmouth two days later, in the evening. At ten o'clock I set out for Mr Peggotty's house. Rain was falling hard and the night was stormy. I saw a light shining inside the house when I arrived.

'What a very pleasant surprise, Mr David!' said Mr Peggotty, with a happy face. 'Sit down, sir.'

The house looked very comfortable indeed. The fire was burning brightly. Peggotty sat in her old chair, as if she had never got up from it. Mrs Gummidge was sitting in her corner of the room. Emily was not there.

'Well, Peggotty, how are you, old woman?' I said, giving her a kiss.

Presently Mr Peggotty looked at the clock and got up. He picked up a candle and put it on the shelf by the window.

'Now the house is lit up. That's a custom of ours,' he said cheerfully. 'Are you wondering why the candle is there? It's for our little Emily. I'll explain. If I'm here when she's coming home, I put the light by the window.' With great laughter he continued, 'That does two things. Emily says, "There's home!" And Emily also says, "My uncle's there!" Because if I'm not there, I never put a light on!'

'You're a baby!' said Peggotty. She was clearly very fond of him, even so.

5 'A great big man like me? Do I look like a baby?' said Mr Peggotty, laughing loudly at the idea. 'Perhaps I am, but not to look at. I don't care. I know when she's married I shall still put the candle by the window. And I shall sit in front of the fire, pretending she'll come.
10 But here she is now!'

Ham came in, but he was alone. He had a large hat on to keep dry in the rain. It was pulled down over his face.

'Where is Emily?' said Mr Peggotty.

15 Ham suddenly saw me sitting in the room. He made a sign with his head as if to say that Emily was outside.

'Mr David, will you come outside a minute? Come and see what Emily and I have got to show you,' he said.

We went out. As I passed him at the door I noticed
20 that his face was white.

'Ham! What's the matter?'

'Mr Davy!' Oh how he cried! He was so unhappy!

I do not know what I thought. I could only look at him.

25 'Ham! Poor, good man, please tell me what's the matter!'

Ham tells the news

'My love, Mr Davy — my hope for the future — the one I would have died for — she's gone!'
30 'Gone!'

I can still remember the terrible look on his face as he turned and looked up to the sky. I will never forget that look.

'You're a man with education,' he said quickly. 'How shall I tell him, Mr Davy?'

I saw the door move. Mr Peggotty had heard everything Ham had said. Never shall I forget Mr Peggotty's face. I remember a great cry. I had a piece of paper in my hand that Ham had given me. Mr Peggotty, his hair wild, and his face and lips quite white, was looking at me.

'Read it,' he said. 'Slowly, please. I don't know whether I can understand anything.'

In the silence, I read with difficulty from a letter, which Emily had written to Ham, thus:

'"You have always loved me more than I deserved, even when I was innocent of all bad thoughts. When you read this letter I shall be far away."'

'"I shall be far away."' Mr Peggotty repeated. 'Stop! Emily far away. Oh!'

'"When I leave my dear home, my dear home; oh, my dear home! — in the morning — I will never come back there unless he marries me. I have done a terrible thing to you and I know you can never forgive me. Oh, you cannot know how much I have suffered, but try to imagine it. I am too wicked to write about myself. Forget how kind and gentle you have all been to me. Forget that we were going to be married. Try

instead to imagine that I died when I was little and was buried somewhere! Love another good girl who can love Uncle and comfort him as I did. Forget me. I'll pray for everyone. My last love and tears are for
5 Uncle!"' That was all.

For a long time after I had stopped reading, Mr Peggotty stood still, looking at me. He did not move, even when I spoke to him. Ham spoke to him.

Slowly, at last, he looked round the room. Then he
10 said, in a low voice, 'Who is the man?'

Ham looked at me, and suddenly I felt a shock. It made me feel weak.

'You suspect someone. Who is he?'

I sat down, and could not speak or see properly.
15 Ham said, 'For a little while, there has been a gentleman round the house, at unusual times.' Ham hesitated, and then continued: 'He was seen with — our poor girl — last night. We thought he had gone, but he was hiding.'

20 If someone had said the house was going to fall on me, I could not have moved.

'Then the stranger was seen in town this morning before dawn. He was making travelling arrangements. Emily was with him. He's the man.'

25 'Oh! don't tell me his name!'

'Mr Davy,' cried Ham in a strange voice, 'it is not your fault, but his name is Steerforth. He's a wicked man!'

Mr Peggotty did not cry and he did not move. Suddenly he seemed to wake up again, as if he had
30 made a decision. 'I'm going to find my poor girl and bring her back,' he said. He asked me whether I was going to London tomorrow. I told him I was ready to go at any time.

'I'll go with you tomorrow, then, Mr Copperfield,' he
35 replied, 'if you don't mind.'

Mr Peggotty visits Mrs Steerforth

When we reached London, we looked for some rooms where Mr Peggotty could sleep. Luckily we found some only two streets away from mine.

He told me that he wanted first to see Mrs Steerforth. 5
I wrote to her that night. I told her as politely as I could what Steerforth had done, and I explained my share in the crime. I said that we would come at two o'clock in the afternoon to see her.

At the arranged time, we arrived at the door. Mrs 10
Steerforth was at home. Rosa Dartle quietly moved from another part of the room and stood behind her chair. I saw immediately that Mrs Steerforth had heard from Steerforth about what he had done.

'Please read this, Mrs Steerforth,' said Mr Peggotty, 15
holding out Emily's letter. 'That's my girl's writing!'

She read it and in a proud, calm way gave it back to him. 'I am quite certain that they can never be married, and never will be,' she said. 'But if there is anything else I can do —' 20

'Are you offering me money for my child who is ruined?'

She changed now, in a moment, and became angry.

'To please my son has been my only purpose in life,' she said. 'Now he has run away suddenly with a 25
worthless girl, and left me! Do you think that this does not wound me?'

Rosa Dartle tried to comfort her, but she would not be comforted.

Then we went away. Mr Peggotty walked slowly and 30
thoughtfully down the hill. He told me he meant to set out on his journey that night. I asked him where he meant to go. He only answered, 'I'm going, sir. I'm going to find my girl.'

9
My Love for Dora

A gain and a loss

All this time I loved Dora more and more. Mr Spenlow told me that it was Dora's birthday in a week's time. He wanted me to come for a little picnic that day.

I think I did everything possible to prepare for this event. At six in the morning I went to the market to buy flowers for Dora in my brightly polished new boots. At ten o'clock I was riding a fine grey horse to Mr Spenlow's house.

When I arrived, I walked in my uncomfortable boots across the garden to Dora. She was sitting under a tree. What a perfect picture she made, surrounded by birds and flowers, in a dress as blue as the sky!

'Oh, thank you, Mr Copperfield! What lovely flowers!' said Dora. 'You will be glad to hear that Miss Murdstone is not here. Isn't that good news?'

I said I was sure it must be good news to her, and I added that all that was good news to her was good news to me.

Mr Spenlow came out of the house and we were ready to set out for the picnic.

I shall never enjoy a ride like that again. There was a great deal of dust, I believe; but I did not see it. I saw only Dora's beauty and felt only my love for her. I could think of nothing and no one but Dora.

Even now, I do not know where we went. I remember a green place, on a hill, with soft grass. There were shady trees and a wonderful view. I was weak with joy. Dora sang. Though the others praised her, I

thought she sang only for me. We had tea, and in the
evening I was as happy as ever.

I was happier still when the party ended and
everyone else went away and I could ride back with the
Spenlows to their house. Mr Spenlow invited me to rest
and eat before returning to London.

When I woke up next morning in London, I decided
to tell Dora how much I loved her. If I did this I would
find out whether she loved me, too. And so I went back
again to the Spenlows' house.

For this purpose I was dressed in expensive clothes.

Dora was painting when I arrived.

'I hope your poor horse was not tired when he got
home last night,' said Dora. She looked at me with her
beautiful eyes. 'It was a long way for him.'

'It was a long way for him,' I agreed. 'He had nothing
to delight him on the journey.'

I began to think I would ask her today.

'Wasn't he fed, poor thing?' said Dora. I began to
think I would not ask her until tomorrow.

'Yes,' I said. 'I mean he did not have the great
happiness I had. I was near you.'

'I don't know why you should call
it happiness,' said Dora, 'but
of course you don't mean
what you say.'

I don't know how I
did it. I did it in a
moment. I held Dora
in my arms. Without
hesitating I made a
fine speech. I told
her how I loved her.
I told her I should
die without her.

Dora bent her head and cried, and trembled. I expressed my feelings even more strongly. I had loved her every minute, day and night, since I first saw her. I always would love her. Lovers had loved before and lovers would love again, but no lover had ever loved as much as I loved Dora.

A little later, Dora and I were sitting quietly beside each other. We were going to be married.

David's aunt comes to stay

One evening I returned from the office to find my front door open. I heard voices inside.

I went in. To my great surprise, I found Peggotty there, with my aunt! My aunt was sitting on a pile of luggage. She was drinking tea which Peggotty had served her.

My aunt had some very bad news. 'I'm ruined, my dear boy,' she said. If the house had fallen into the river I would not have had a greater shock.

Then, quite calmly, she told me that all her money had gone. There was nothing left, except the cottage, and the things she had brought with her. She told me that Peggotty had been begging her to take some of her money, but of course she would not think of it.

My aunt had heard about my love for Dora. She did not seem to be very happy about it, and called us 'Poor little children.'

'I know we are young, and we have little experience, Aunt,' I explained. 'But we love each other truly, I am sure. I do not know what I would do if Dora loved anybody else or stopped loving me. And I should go mad if I thought I could ever love anyone else, or stop loving her.'

'David!' said my aunt, smiling sadly. 'You are blind! Blind! Blind!'

I was unhappy without knowing why; I felt as though I had just lost something and I was worried.

The night seemed very long. My aunt went to sleep, but she could not rest. I heard her several times walking around. I stopped trying to sleep, myself, and at last saw the sun shining through the window.

I dressed myself as quickly as I could, and told Peggotty to look after Miss Trotwood. I went for a walk. I was trying to imagine my aunt without any money.

Mr Wickfield has changed

Soon after this I met Agnes again. She had come to London with her father — and Uriah Heep. I took her to my rooms to see my aunt.

My aunt was very pleased to see Agnes, and welcomed us cheerfully. We talked about my aunt's losses. I told them that I meant to find a job in addition to my work at Spenlow and Jorkins. Agnes said that the headmaster of my old school, Dr Strong, was in London, and looking for a secretary. I sat down to write to him immediately.

While I was writing, Agnes was cleaning and tidying every part of my rooms. I watched her, and thought how much she did in her calm and quiet way. Then there was a knock at the door.

Agnes, whose face was suddenly pale, said, 'I think Father has come.'

I opened the door; Mr Wickfield came in and Uriah Heep came in behind him. I had not seen Mr Wickfield for a long time, and his appearance shocked me. He looked much older. His face was red and he looked unhealthy. His hands trembled. But something shocked me more than all this. He was clearly absolutely controlled by Uriah Heep. This respectable, kind gentleman obeyed the mean, twisting Uriah.

Agnes softly said to him, 'Father! Here is Miss Trotwood — and David. We have not seen them for a long time!' And then Mr Wickfield shook hands with my aunt and with me. I saw Uriah smile an ugly smile.

5 Agnes saw too, for she stepped away from him.

He twisted himself about in such an unpleasant way that my aunt became very annoyed. She said in a cross voice, 'What's he doing? Don't twist like that, sir! If you're a worm, behave like one. If you're a man, control

10 your body, sir!'

Mr Heep was rather frightened by my aunt's fierce speech. Afterwards he spoke to me quietly so my aunt

15 would not hear.

'I know that Miss Trotwood has a bad temper, although she is an excellent lady,' he said. 'I only came to ask whether there was anything we could do in the present situation. Mother or I, or Wickfield and Heep,

20 would be very glad to help.'

'I quite agree with what Uriah says,' said Mr Wickfield. He said this in a dull, obedient voice.

'To be trusted in this way is my reward, Master Copperfield!' said Uriah. I saw the same ugly smile on his face again, and saw how he watched me.

I make some decisions

The next day I went to see Dr Strong, who was willing for me to work as his secretary. He generously offered me a good salary. I knew it would be very useful to my aunt and me in our new situation. We decided I should begin next morning at seven o'clock. Our plans being satisfactorily arranged, we went into Dr Strong's house. Here he gave me some tea before I left to go home.

I felt as though I had started a new life. I wanted to do something else as well, and decided to find out whether Traddles could help me. I had heard that many important and successful men had worked as reporters for newspapers when they were young. Traddles now told me that I did not have the skill needed for this work. This was a special way of writing very quickly. He said it was as difficult as learning six different foreign languages.

'I am very grateful to you, my dear Traddles,' I said. 'I'll begin tomorrow. I'll buy a book with a good plan for learning this art. Traddles, my dear lad, I'll learn it.'

Traddles was very surprised. But he did not know that I had to prove to my aunt that I was responsible, and seriously in love with Dora.

'I had no idea you had such a determined character, Copperfield!' he said.

Suddenly he took a letter out of his pocket, and said, 'This matter has really made me forget Mr Micawber completely!'

The letter was addressed to me. It was from Mr Micawber. He said that the family was about to leave London. They were going to live in a smaller town. He invited Traddles and me to have dinner at his house
5 that evening.

Traddles and I left immediately.

When we reached the Micawbers I saw that everything that belonged to the family had been packed already.

10 I spoke eagerly to Mrs Micawber about the change.

'I know, my dear Mr Copperfield, that we may be sacrificing ourselves by going to a dull town. But surely, Mr Copperfield, if it is a sacrifice for me, it is a far greater one for a man of Mr Micawber's abilities,'
15 said Mrs Micawber.

'Oh! Which town are you going to?' I asked.

Mr Micawber had been serving us all with drinks out of a large jug that had not been made for this purpose. The drink tasted like a mixture of tea and
20 coffee. He now replied, 'We are going to Canterbury. In fact, my dear Copperfield, I have made an arrangement with our friend Heep. I am going to help and serve him as his personal clerk.'

I stared at Mr Micawber, who greatly enjoyed seeing
25 my surprise.

10
Dora and I are Married

The accident

My new life had lasted for more than a week. I was more determined than ever to prove myself really useful to my aunt in our difficult situation.

Nor did I forget my decision to learn to be a reporter. Traddles suggested that he should read speeches to me to write down. I accepted his suggestion. Every night, for a long time, we worked together, after I came home from Dr Strong's.

As a result of so much good practice, I was soon able to write as quickly as Traddles read the speeches to me. I really did work very hard.

One day, when I went to the office, I found Mr Spenlow at the door. He was looking very angry. He did not say, 'Good morning,' in his usual friendly way. Instead he politely requested me to go with him to a coffee shop.

When I saw Miss Murdstone waiting for us there, I realized that they must have found out about me and Dora.

Miss Murdstone opened her bag. She took out a parcel of letters, tied together with a lovely piece of blue ribbon. They were my letters to Dora.

I tried to explain how much I loved Dora, but Mr Spenlow interrupted. 'You are both very young,' he said. 'Let us have no more nonsense. Please give me the letters that Miss Spenlow has written to you, so that we can throw them into the fire, Mr Copperfield.'

No. I could not agree to that.

'In that case, Mr Copperfield,' said Mr Spenlow, 'I must try to influence my daughter myself.'

He told me later that I need not be anxious about his daughter's happiness. He had told her that this affair was nonsense. His family was a wealthy one, so he wanted to choose a rich husband of high rank for his
5   daughter.

I went to bed that night with no hope.

I got up on Saturday morning without hope, and I went out without hope. I went straight to the office. When I reached the office all the clerks were there, but
10   nobody was doing any work.

'This is a terrible news, Mr Copperfield,' said the chief clerk as I entered. He then told me that Mr Spenlow had died on the way home from work the previous evening. He had been driving alone, and had
15   fallen from his carriage. When his servants found him he had been dead for some time.

I was so surprised that I could not speak.

Dora's aunts

Dora had two aunts who lived in Putney. These two
20   ladies now suggested taking Dora to live with them. She had nowhere else to go, and she had no money of her own. Mr Spenlow, it seemed, had been a very poor man when he died.

The aunts wrote to say that I should visit them. I
25   wrote back to accept their invitation, and to tell them how much I loved Dora. Then, on the important day, and taking Traddles with me, I walked to Putney.

We were led into a quiet, neat sitting room. Two dry little old ladies were sitting there, waiting for us. I
30   noticed that one sister was six or eight years older than the other. The younger one seemed to be in control; she had my letter in her hand. The other sister sat with her arms folded.

The sister who was holding my letter, began. 'Mr Copperfield, my sister Clarissa and I believe you are a young gentleman with a good and honourable character,' she said.

'You ask the permission of my sister Lavinia and myself to visit Miss Dora,' said Miss Clarissa. 'My sister and I have considered this letter very carefully. We are sure you think you like Miss Dora very much.'

I replied that nobody ever loved anybody as much as I loved Dora. In fact, I usually told people this when I had the chance.

Miss Lavinia read my letter again through her glasses. Both sisters had little, bright, round, shining eyes, which were like birds' eyes. They had a little short, quick way of moving. They were rather like birds altogether. Miss Lavinia then continued, 'We think the best plan is to test your love for Dora, Mr Copperfield. Therefore we will allow you to visit her here.'

'I shall never forget your kindness, dear ladies!' I cried.

'Sister Clarissa,' said Miss Lavinia, 'the rest is for you to arrange.'

Miss Clarissa unfolded her arms for the first time. She then told me that I would be invited to dinner, every Sunday, at three o'clock, and for tea, at half past six in the evening, on two other days every week.

When I heard this I was delighted. I bowed respectfully to both ladies.

Miss Lavinia then stood up, and requested me to follow her. I obeyed, trembling, and was led into another room. There I found my Dora.

A wedding

Let me stop now, and consider an important period of my life.

I was twenty-one and no longer a boy, but a man. I had learnt the art of being a reporter. I was earning quite a good salary from it. I worked with eleven other men for a newspaper. My dear friend Traddles was working for the same newspaper, doing the same kind of work. I had begun to write short stories and had had the courage to send several pieces to a magazine. Soon I was being paid as an author. Altogether, my situation was very good.

I was going to be married to Dora! Miss Lavinia and Miss Clarissa had given their permission. They were very busy and excited planning the wedding. Peggotty had come to London to help. Her chief job seemed to be to clean everything again and again.

My dreams were coming true.

'I tell you, I am almost as pleased as if I were going to be married myself,' said Traddles.

Agnes came from Canterbury. I met her, and was able to see her beautiful face again.

Still I did not believe it. In two days' time I was to be married. We had a delightful evening, and were very happy. But I could not believe it yet.

Next day we all went to see the house. It was our house, Dora's and mine; but I was quite unable to imagine myself as its owner. It was a beautiful little house, with everything bright and new. There were flowers and leaves on the curtains that looked as though they had just grown. All Dora's things were already in the right places.

I went home, my thoughts more mixed up than ever, to a room I was staying in nearby. I got up very early in the morning to go and fetch my aunt.

I had never seen her in such a state. She wore a light blue silk dress and a white hat. Peggotty was ready to go to the church, too.

We drove along in an open carriage. I felt a kind of pity for the unlucky people who were working and doing their ordinary jobs.

We came to the church door. The rest was really a dream.

I dreamt they came in with Dora. The clerk appeared, and the wedding began.

I remember Miss Lavinia cried first.

I remember Dora and I knelt, side by side; the wedding followed. I remember we all looked at each other with smiles and tears when it was over.

I remember walking out of the church, with my sweet wife holding my arm, and feeling so proud. I was so happy I hardly saw the people, but they whispered, as we passed, what a pretty little wife she was.

We had a wedding feast with many fine things to eat and drink.

Then Dora was ready; then Dora realized again and again, to her surprise, that she had forgotten one more thing. I remember everyone running all over the house to fetch things for her.

And finally she waved her little hand, and we went away at last.

We drove away together, and I woke up from my dream. I believed everything at last. My dear, dear little wife whom I loved so much, was sitting beside me!

Our life together

My pretty Dora and I did not know how to manage a house. I don't think any two young people could know less than we did. We had a servant, of course, and she looked after the house for us.

But she worried us a great deal. She was the subject of our first little quarrel. Of course, we were soon friends again, and we agreed that our first little quarrel would be our last. We would never have another in our lives.

Dora told me, soon afterwards, that she intended to manage the house very well, so she bought a book to learn how to cook. She made a great attempt 'to be good', as she called it. She also bought a huge book to write down the money we spent. She would copy two or three things in it, and then she would look up so hopelessly and say, 'The numbers won't come right. They make my head ache so much. And they won't do anything I want.'

Then I would say, 'Let us try together. Let me show you, Dora.'

Dora would watch very carefully, for perhaps five minutes. Soon she would become very tired and would begin twisting my hair round her fingers; or considering how I looked with my shirt collar turned up.

Thus I managed the problems and affairs of our life, and had no partner to help me.

Dora was rarely unhappy, which pleased me, but she was not strong. She looked very pretty and was very merry, but the little feet that used to dance around so quickly gradually became dull and still.

I began to carry her downstairs every morning and upstairs every night. Sometimes when I picked her up I noticed that she was lighter. Slowly I began to understand that my little Dora was very ill indeed. I felt then that my whole life was blank and dead.

11
Emily's Return, Uriah's Crimes

'He used all his power to trick me'

Some months had passed since the beginning of Dora's illness. I was walking in the garden, bent with sadness. By chance, thinking of many different things, I looked up from the garden to the road. I saw a person coming eagerly towards me. It was Mr Peggotty, looking old and ill, but clearly in a state of excitement.

'My girl Emily is alive, sir!' he said, his eyes shining brightly. 'Can you come with me to see her?'

My answer was to walk out of the garden to him, immediately. Without a word being spoken we hurried to one of the dark streets of London. Here the houses had once been fine; now they were in very poor condition and let as single rooms. Entering one of these, he signalled to me to follow him up the broken stairs.

Just as we reached Emily's room we heard a woman's voice speaking loudly and angrily. It was not Emily's, but to my great surprise, I recognized it. It was the voice of Miss Dartle. Mr Peggotty and I waited outside Emily's door, which was partly open, and listened.

'I do not care if he is not home,' Rosa Dartle was saying angrily. 'I came to see you.'

'Me?' replied a soft voice.

When I heard that voice my joy was great. It was Emily's voice.

'Yes,' replied Miss Dartle, 'I have come to see the girl who ran away with him. The bold companion of James Steerforth. Do you ever think about the home you have ruined?'

'Oh, every day, and every night I think of it!' cried Emily. 'Oh, home, home!'

'Your home!' shouted Rosa Dartle. She almost screamed the words. 'Do you imagine that I care for your home, you worm! I speak about his home — where I live. There is reason for sadness in a lady's house, where you would not be allowed to work in the kitchen! You are a piece of rubbish picked up on the shore. You are fit to be used for a while, and then thrown back to your original place!'

'No! No!' cried Emily. 'I do not defend my actions. But I know well, and he knows well, that he used all his power to trick me. And I believed him, and trusted him, and loved him!'

'You love him? You?' Miss Dartle cried. 'And dare you say that to me, with your shameful lips? Why don't they whip girls like you? If I could order you to be whipped to death, I would.'

Slowly, very slowly, she began to laugh.

Her laughter was worse than her terrible anger.

'I came here to see what you were like. I was curious. I am satisfied. But — I have something else to say. Listen, for I will do what I say. Hide yourself somewhere; somewhere you cannot be found. Find some secret life, or better, a secret death. If you live here, I'll tell everyone what you have done!'

Rosa Dartle opened the door and walked quickly past us. She did not seem to notice that we were there.

Mr Peggotty sighed with relief. He rushed into the room.

'Uncle!'

A terrible cry followed the word. Looking in, I saw Mr Peggotty holding Emily in his arms. She had fainted.

'Mr Davy,' he said. 'I thank Heaven my dream has come true! I thank God; he guided me to my darling.'

Having said this, he picked
her up in his arms and
carried her, absolutely still
and unconscious,
down the stairs.

Mr Peggotty tells the story

The next morning while it was early, Mr Peggotty came
to my house, and told me what had happened.

'That snake, James Steerforth, took her away to Italy
where they lived in a house by the sea. She could not   10
speak the language, and she had no friends. She did not
know how to get back home. She was Steerforth's
prisoner there. Then, one day, she decided to run away.
She found her way to France. She worked there as a
servant to some travelling ladies. Then she came to   15
England, landing at Dover.

'She reached London.' Mr Peggotty was whispering
now. 'She had never lived here in her life. She was
alone — with no money at all — young — pretty — and
she came to London. But almost as soon as she arrived   20
she found someone to help her. She was a good woman,
who told Emily she could find her work, and
somewhere to stay for the night. She told her she would
ask secretly about me the next day.'

I gave a cry of joy.

'She looked after my Emily,' said Mr Peggotty. 'Emily was very tired and slept till late the next day. Then the woman went out to search for me.'

He stopped speaking. We were all silent, thinking about his story, until I spoke.

'Have you decided what you are going to do now, my friend?'

'Yes, Mr Davy,' said Mr Peggotty smiling hopefully. 'I have told Emily there are great countries far from here. We must live abroad. We will go to Australia to start a new life. Emily will stay with me until we go on our journey. Poor child, she needs peace and rest so that she can recover.

'There is one more thing, Mr Davy,' said he. 'I wrote a letter to Ham, while I was out, telling him about the situation. I said I would come tomorrow to see Yarmouth for the last time, and say goodbye.'

'And would you like me to go with you?' said I.

'I would, Mr Davy,' he replied. 'I know the sight of you would cheer them all up a bit!'

I willingly agreed to go with him. So next morning we set off for Yarmouth.

We went straight to the old boat. They were all there, waiting for us in the neat kitchen. Mr Peggotty told them everything. Both Peggotty and Mrs Gummidge wiped the tears from their eyes. Ham went out 'to take a walk on the beach'; he wanted to be alone.

Peggotty led me to my little room. She told me she thought Ham would never be happy again. Sometimes, she said, in the evening, he talked about their old life. He would mention Emily as a child, but he never mentioned her as a woman.

When I spoke to Ham he was very sad. 'There is something I would like you to say or write to Emily for me,' he said. 'Ask her to forgive me for persuading her to marry me. Often, I think that if I hadn't asked her to marry me, she would have told me what worried her. And I could have saved her. You know how much I love her still.' 5

I promised I would tell Emily what he had said.

The wickedness of Uriah Heep

Soon after I returned to London I received a letter from Mr Micawber. He was in Canterbury and asked me to meet him there. I was even more curious when I read 10 that he wanted me to come with Traddles, and my aunt.

We arrived at the old house the next morning. Mr Micawber greeted us, and took us to meet Uriah Heep. Opening the door of what had been Mr Wickfield's office, he said, in a loud voice, 'Miss Trotwood, Mr 15 David Copperfield, and Mr Thomas Traddles!'

Our visit was clearly a complete surprise to Uriah Heep.

At that moment Agnes entered. I could see that she had been anxious and troubled, but she was still quiet 20 and beautiful. And then Traddles, who, unnoticed by anyone, had gone out, returned, bringing Uriah's mother with him.

Traddles then told Uriah that he had been ordered to act as Mr Wickfield's lawyer, and Mr Micawber had 25 been helping him.

Mr Micawber took an important looking letter from his coat pocket. He opened it, looked round at all of us, and began to read.

'"I began a careful search which lasted more than 30 twelve months,"' he read out slowly, '"and I accuse Uriah Heep of these crimes."'

We all held our breath, I think. I am sure Uriah did.

Mr Micawber continued, '"First, Heep persuaded Mr Wickfield to sign important business papers. He pretended that they were quite unimportant. He persuaded Mr Wickfield to give him power to take a certain amount of money. Uriah said the money was to meet business costs which he did not really have to pay. He made his dishonest deed appear to be Mr Wickfield's. And he has used this situation ever since to worry him and to control him.

'"Second, Heep has purposely signed business papers with Mr Wickfield's name." I am sure he has done this many times, and in one case I can prove it; I have the paper in my pocket.

'"Third, I can now show Heep planned to force Mr Wickfield to give up his share in the business, his money, his house, even his furniture to him."'

During the last few minutes Mrs Heep had been crying to her son to give up. He said, with a fierce look, 'What do you want me to do?'

'I will tell you what must be done,' said Traddles. 'First, the false papers must be given to me. Then you must give back all the money you have taken. We must keep all the books and papers and all the money here. And you must stay in your own room, and not speak or write to anyone.'

'I won't do what you ask!' cried Uriah.   5

'Then the prison is a safer place to keep you. Copperfield, will you go and get two policemen?'

I moved towards the door. Mrs Heep began to cry again. She prayed on her knees to Agnes to help them. She was half mad with fear for her dear son.   10

'Stop!' Uriah growled, and wiped his hot face with his hand. 'Mother, stop making so much noise. Let them have the papers. Go and fetch them!'

Mrs Heep was not difficult to manage. She not only returned with the papers, but with a box of money,   15
too.

'Good!' said Traddles. 'Now, Mr Heep, you can go to your room.'

Uriah, without looking up from the ground, crept across the room. He paused at the door and said,   20
'Copperfield, I have always hated you. You've always judged me unfairly. Micawber, you're a cruel man, and I'll punish you for this.'

Later, Traddles told us that he had recovered all of my aunt's property from Uriah. She was very pleased,   25
and very grateful, as she was soon able to show.

Miss Trotwood's suggestion to the Micawbers

Agnes had to return to her father, and someone had to prevent Uriah from escaping. So Traddles remained for the latter purpose, and my aunt and I went home with   30
Mr Micawber.

His house was not far away. He rushed in and kissed the whole family. Then my aunt was introduced.

'Is this all your family?' said my aunt. 'Are all these your children?'

'Madam, they are indeed!' replied Mr Micawber, 'and to find a way to look after all of them is indeed
5   very difficult.'

'Have you never considered going abroad?' asked my aunt.

'Madam,' replied Mr Micawber, 'that was my great hope when I was young. It is still my hope now that I
10 am older.'

'You have done us a great service, Mr Micawber,' said my aunt. Now we can show our thanks by giving you the money you need to go abroad.'

'I could not receive it as a present,' said Mr
15 Micawber, both eager and frightened. 'But if I could pay it back with a little more —'

'You can do that, and will,' said my aunt. 'David knows some people going to Australia soon. Why shouldn't you go in the same ship?'

20   'There is one question only that I wish to ask, dear madam,' said Mrs Micawber. 'Is the state of the country suitable for a man of Mr Micawber's abilities? Would he have a chance to improve his position in the world?'

'A man who behaves himself well and works hard
25 can find no greater opportunities anywhere,' said my aunt.

'Behaves himself well and works hard,' repeated Mrs Micawber. 'Exactly. Clearly Australia is the right place for Mr Micawber.'

12
Sad Losses, Happy Endings

Dora asks to see Agnes

Here I must pause. I was with Dora again, in our
cottage. I cannot remember how long she had been
ill in weeks or months, but to me her illness seemed to
have lasted a long, long time.   5

I was sitting by her bed, in the evening. We were
silent, and Dora was smiling. I no longer carried her up
and down stairs now. She lay on her bed all day.

'David!'

'My dear Dora!'   10

'Are you very lonely when you go downstairs, now?'

'Of course I am, my own love, when I see your empty
chair.'

'My empty chair! And you really miss me, David?
You miss poor, silly, stupid Dora?'   15

'My love, there is no one on this earth I could miss
so much.'

'Oh, husband! I am so glad, yet so sorry! Just give
Agnes my love and tell her I want very, very much to
see her. There is nothing else left to wish for.'   20

A great loss

A few days later Agnes arrived from Canterbury. She
had been with us for a whole day and an evening. Later
that evening I was alone with Dora, in our room
upstairs.   25

'I am going to speak to you, David. I am going to say
something I have often thought of saying lately. You
won't mind, will you?' she said, with a gentle look.

'No, my darling.'

'Perhaps you have often had the same thought. David, dear, I am afraid I was too young. I was such a silly little girl! I do not think I was fit to be a wife.'

'Oh, Dora, love! You were as fit to be a wife as I was to be a husband. We have been very happy, my sweet Dora.'

'I was very, very happy. But this is the best end. When you go downstairs, ask Agnes to come up to me. While I speak to her, let no one come in. I want to speak to Agnes quite alone.'

I promised that she would come immediately.

Agnes was downstairs and I went into the sitting room. I gave her the message. She went out, leaving me alone.

I sat down by the fire. I thought about every little quarrel between me and Dora and knew how sorry I felt for ever having made Dora cry. How the time went, I did not know. Then I saw Agnes at the door, looking at me, and saw the pity and unhappiness in her gentle face.

'Agnes?'

Then I knew that everything was over. Darkness seemed to come all round me and for a while I could remember nothing.

Two more deaths

I cannot clearly remember when we decided I should go abroad. I waited only for what Mr Micawber called 'the end of Heep' and for the Peggottys and Micawbers to leave. I decided to make one last trip to Yarmouth, before their boat sailed.

When I reached Yarmouth the weather was very bad, and I heard people shouting that there had been a wreck. I hurried towards the beach. There was a large crowd of people there. I pushed my way through to the front and was soon facing the wild sea.

I could hardly hear anything except the wind and the roaring sea and I could see little but the white tops of the great waves. Then I saw the ship, close to us! It was badly broken, with sails and ropes twisted together. Slowly it turned towards us. I could clearly see her sailors working with axes. One person, with long, untidy hair, I noticed especially. He had a red seaman's hat in his hand. We all saw him wave it. The action reminded me of someone who had once been a dear friend.

The ship was breaking in half. The waves were too wild for any human work to continue for long. The wreck sank suddenly down into the water, and then rose again to the surface. In that short moment, two men drowned.

Then I saw Ham come rushing through the people to the front. I ran to him.

'Mr Davy,' he said, seizing me by both hands. 'If I die now, I die. Heaven protect you, and all of you. Get me ready! I'm going!'

Ham tied a rope around himself and began pushing himself through the stormy water to the wreck. As he went a high, green wave, like a huge hill of water, moved towards the shore. He leapt into it, and then he, and the ship, had gone!

I saw his body in the sea. I was running to the place where they were pulling him in. They pulled him to my feet. He was carried to the nearest house and a doctor was found. But he had been beaten too badly by the great wave. Ham, that generous man was dead.

I sat beside the bed, when there was no more hope. Suddenly, a man whispered my name.

'Sir, will you come here?' he said, with tears on his grey, pale face.

He led me to the shore. He led me to that part of it where Emily and I had looked for shells. Then I saw
5   him lying with his head on his arm, as I had often seen him lie at school. This time, however, he would never wake again.

Sad goodbyes

10   One thing I had to do. I had to prevent those who were going away from knowing what had happened.

I went back to London. I found that Mr Peggotty and Emily had left their house early, at five o'clock, to go to the ship. In the afternoon my old nurse, Peggotty, and I
15   went to say goodbye. We saw the ship in the river, ready to sail.

Mr Peggotty was waiting for us on deck. We spoke quietly for a while, but it was soon time to leave. I shook his hand; I held Peggotty, who was crying, by the
20   arm, and we hurried away.

We saw Mr Micawber. I told him about the terrible events that had happened the night before. He promised to make sure Mr Peggotty did not hear the news. He appeared to be cheerful. He expected his family would have a good life at last. On deck I said goodbye to Mrs Micawber. The last thing she said to me was that she would never leave Mr Micawber.

We left the ship. As the wind filled the sails, the ship began to move. Everyone in the boats gave three loud cheers. Those on the ship joined in and the sound could be heard long after the cheering had stopped. I had a great feeling of happiness when I heard the sound and watched the crowd waving hats and handkerchiefs. And then I saw her!

Then I saw Emily, standing beside her uncle, leaning on his arm and looking weak. He showed her eagerly where we were; and she saw us, and waved her last goodbye to me.

Agnes

I went away from England. I did not know, even then, how great the shock had been. I was sad because my wife, who was so like a child, had died so young.

For many months I travelled. Sometimes I went from place to place, unable to rest. Sometimes I stayed a long time in one place. I came one evening down to a valley where I was to stay for the night. I found a packet of letters waiting for me. I wandered out of the village to read them while my supper was being prepared. I opened the packet in my hand and read Agnes's writing.

She gave me no advice. She only told me, in her own quiet manner, that she trusted me. I read her letter many times.

I was away for three years. In that time I was sad and lonely, far away from home. Home was very dear to me. Agnes was dear to me too, but she was not my wife, and never would be, I thought to myself. She might have been at one time but that time was past.

I returned to London on a cold winter's evening. I saw more mud and snow in a minute than I had seen in a year.

I had expected some changes in the lives of my friends. My aunt had gone back to live in Dover. Traddles was married, and happy with his family. I should not call Heep a friend, but Heep was in prison. Rosa Dartle was so lonely she had stayed to look after Mrs Steerforth. The latter was a sad, but still proud, old lady. Soon I was on my way to Dover to see my aunt, and then, on the following morning, I rode to Canterbury, to see Agnes.

When we met I held her to me, and for a little while we were both silent. Presently we sat down, beside each other.

Her face, like a saint's, was looking at me. This was the welcome I had dreamt of for years. I tried to tell her how important she had been to me; but my love and joy were so great I could not speak.

With her own sweet, peaceful manner she spoke to me about Emily whom she had visited secretly, many times, while Emily was in London. She spoke to me gently about Dora's grave.

'And now, Agnes, tell me about your own life,' I said presently.

'What shall I tell you?' she answered. 'My father is well; we are no longer worried, and our home is safe again. That is all, dear David. But there is one thing I must say.'

She laid her gentle hands on my shoulders and looked at me calmly.

'Tell me, my dear.'

'I have loved you all my life!'

We were married in two weeks. Traddles and my aunt, Mr Wickfield and Dr Strong were the only guests at our quiet wedding. We left them and drove away together, joyfully.

'Dearest husband!' said Agnes, 'I must tell you something. It is about the night when Dora died. She told you to fetch me. She told me that she was leaving something for me. Can you think what it was?'

I believed I could. I drew the wife who had so long loved me, closer to my side.

'She told me her last request.'

'And it was — '

'That only I would be your wife.'

And Agnes laid her head on my shoulder and cried. I cried with her.

The end

And now this story ends. I remember those times once more — for the last time — before I close this book.

I remember myself, with Agnes at my side, travelling along the road of life.

I remember my aunt, an old woman, but standing straight. She still walked six miles at a time in cold weather. Peggotty was always with her, Peggotty, my good old nurse. I remember her with her sewing,
5   wearing glasses, sitting very close to the lamp. Her cheeks and arms were old and dry now; they were red and hard when I was a child. I used to wonder why the birds did not try to eat them instead of apples.

I remember an old lady, whose face showed she was
10 once proud and beautiful. She suddenly cried in a terrible voice: 'Rosa, come to me. He is dead!' Rosa knelt at her feet and was kind to her sometimes. Sometimes she quarrelled with her, telling her fiercely, 'I loved him better than you ever did!' I have
15 remembered all these people and thought about them often.

I met my dear old Traddles again, working as a lawyer. I had dinner with him and his family on his wife's birthday. He told me all the good things that had
20 happened to him.

And now I will close this book, and forget these faces. But one face, shining on me like a light from heaven, I will never forget. That face remains. I turn my head and see it, peaceful beside me. My lamp is nearly
25 out, and I have written so long it is nearly morning. But my dear wife, without whom I could do nothing, is with me.

Questions and Activities

1 An Unhappy Childhood

Circle the right words to say what happened.

Mr Murdstone became David's (1) **father/uncle**. He was not a (2) **cruel/kind** man. David knew he would be beaten if he (3) **pleased/displeased** him. Then Mr Murdstone's (4) **elder/younger** sister came. She was a (5) **cross-looking/sad-looking** woman. She had (6) **fair/dark** hair, just like (7) **David's mother/ her brother**. The Murdstones wanted to send David to (8) **school/Yarmouth**. They made his mother (9) **disagree/agree** with their plans.

2 Away from Home

Who did these things? Fill in the gaps with the names from the box. You can use some names more than once.

Mr Creakle	Peggotty	Tommy Traddles
Mr Mell	Steerforth	

1 _____ gave David a purse with seven shillings in it.

2 _____ put a notice on David's back.

3 ▨▨▨▨▨▨▨▨▨▨ introduced David to all the other boys.

4 ▨▨▨▨▨▨▨▨ helped David to buy a feast for the boys.

5 ▨▨▨▨▨▨▨ liked to strike David every time he walked past him.

6 ▨▨▨▨▨▨▨▨ called Steerforth 'mean and dishonourable'.

7 ▨▨▨▨▨▨▨ said that Mr Mell was not a gentleman.

8 ▨▨▨▨▨▨▨ cried because Mr Mell was leaving the school.

3 I Start Work

Put the letters of these words in the right order. The first one has been done for you.

David thought Emily was (1) **tripeter** _(prettier)_ than ever. After

tea, David told the (2) **limfya** about Salem House, and

about Steerforth. He said that Steerforth was a very

(3) **sohamned**, noble young man. Little Emily was

(4) **nigstilen** with full attention, her eyes shining like

(5) weslje. David stopped, (6) **prissured**. Then they all

(7) **hugaled**. Emily was (8) **daamesh**, and hid her face.

4 **Betsy Trotwood**

Complete the crossword puzzle. In the centre you will see the name of someone who helped David.

David walked to (1). He asked some (2) about his aunt, but no one answered him (3). He was hungry and (4), and his (5) were dirty. He found his aunt's cottage and told her about his (6)'s (7). Then he (8) into tears. In the morning, David's aunt said she had (9) to the Murdstones. A (10) later, they came. They said David was very (11), and behaved like a (12). David's aunt said David's new (13) would be with her.

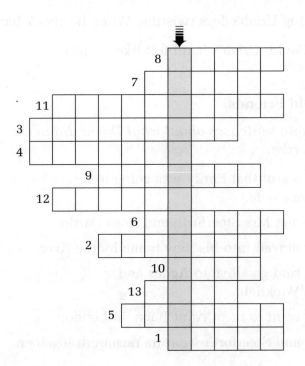

5 The Humble Mr Heep

There are eight mistakes in this paragraph. Find and correct them.

Uriah could not speak like other people; he could only make his mouth wider. He had wet feet, which he was always rubbing together as if he was trying to make them dry and cold. Often he wiped them secretly on his trousers. He had a way of hissing like a snake when he spoke. This was very beautiful. David could not listen to Uriah because he was watching Uriah's legs twisting. When he shook hands with David, Uriah's hand felt like a snake.

6 Old Friends

Put these sentences about what David did in the right order.

1 He learnt that Emily was going to be
   Ham's wife.   ☐

2 He met Mrs Steerforth and Rosa Dartle.   ☐

3 He moved into his new home by the river.   ☐

4 He said goodbye to Agnes and
   Mr Wickfield.   ☐

5 He went to meet Aunt Betsy in London.   ☐

6 He and Steerforth went to Yarmouth together. ☐

7 He met Steerforth in London and went ☐
to stay with him.

8 He introduced Steerforth to Peggotty's ☐
family.

7 The New Partner

Circle the right words to say what happened.

David received a (1) **present/letter/visit** from Agnes.

She told him that Uriah was to be her father's

(2) **partner/clerk/lawyer**. Uriah was very

(3) **skilful/stupid/kind**. He had taken advantage

of her father, and her father was now very

(4) **angry/happy/afraid**. Agnes said that she suspected

(5) **worse/better/good** things. She knew that Uriah's

(6) **wealth/power/goodness** was very great.

8 Emily Leaves Home

*The underlined sentences are all in the wrong
paragraph. Which paragraph should they go in?*

1 Rosa was angry that Steerforth had such
power over her. <u>She said that she would not
return unless Steerforth married her.</u> When
Steerforth laughed, she became angry again. ☐

2 In her letter, Emily told Ham to forget her.
<u>She sang a song that expressed all she felt
and thought.</u> She asked Ham to find another
good girl to love. ☐

3 David saw that Mrs Steerforth knew everything. <u>She had been seen in town that morning with Steerforth.</u> She thought that her son had run away with a worthless girl.

4 Ham knew who Emily had gone away with. <u>She was quite certain that the pair could not be married.</u> Mr Peggotty decided to find her and bring her back.

9 My Love for Dora

Who said these things? Use the names from the box.

Aunt Betsy	Mr Micawber	Traddles
David	Mr Wickfield	Uriah Heep

1 'I should go mad if I thought I could ever love anyone else.'

2 'If you're a man, control your body, sir!'

3 'I quite agree with what Uriah says.'

4 'To be trusted in this way is my reward.'

5 'I had no idea you had such a determined character.'

6 'I am going to serve Heep as his personal clerk.'

10 Dora and I are Married

Match the beginning of each sentence to the right ending.

1 Mr Spenlow said he was from a wealthy family, so he •

2 Dora's aunts decided to test David's love for her, so they •

3 David worked for a newspaper and as an author, so his •

4 David could not believe he would marry Dora, so the •

5 Dora did not know how to manage the house, so she •

6 David realized that Dora was very ill, so he •

• **a** situation was very good.

• **b** bought a cook book.

• **c** began to feel blank and dead.

• **d** wanted a rich husband for Dora.

• **e** wedding felt like a dream.

• **f** allowed him to visit her.

11 Emily's Return, Uriah's Crimes

Which of these sentences are true? What is wrong with the false ones?

	T	F
1 Uriah gave Mr Wickfield some unimportant papers to sign.	☐	☐
2 Mr Wickfield knew the papers were very important.	☐	☐

3 Uriah made his dishonesty appear to be Mr Wickfield's. □ □

4 Mr Wickfield used the situation to control Uriah. □ □

5 Heep signed papers with David's name. □ □

6 Uriah planned to make Mr Wickfield give him everything. □ □

12 Sad Losses, Happy Endings

Fill in the gaps with the words from the box.

advice	dear	many	packet	valley
child	lonely	months	trusted	wandered

David went away from England. He was sad because Dora, who was so like a (1)　　　　　　had died. For many (2)　　　　　　, he travelled. One evening, he came down to a (3)　　　　　　and found a (4)　　　　　　of letters waiting for him. He (5)　　　　　　out of the village to read them. In her letter, Agnes gave him no (6)　　　　　　but told him that she (7)　　　　　　him. He read it (8)　　　　　　times. David was sad and (9)　　　　　　, far away from home. Home, and Agnes, were very (10)　　　　　　to him.

Book Report

Now write a book report to display in the library or your classroom. These questions will help you.

Title

Type What type of story is your book?

- Adventure
- Classic
- Crime
- Detective story
- Fairy tale
- Horror and suspense

- Mystery
- Play
- Romance
- Science fiction and fantasy
- Short story
- Others

Characters	Who are the main characters in the book?
Main characters	Describe the main characters. What do they look like? What are they like?
Story	What is the story about? Remember not to give the ending away!
My comments	What did you think of the story? Did you enjoy it? Would you recommend this book to your classmates?

Visit the website and download the book report template
www.oupchina.com.hk/elt/oper

STARTER

The Ant and the Grasshopper and Other Stories by Aesop

Retold by David Foulds
Includes:
  The Ant and the Grasshopper
  The Dog, the Cock and the Fox
  The Wind and the Sun
  The Jackdaw and the Doves
  The Boy Who Cried Wolf
  The Horses and the Deer
  The Ass and the Wolf
  The Hare and the Tortoise

The Brave Little Tailor and Other Stories by the Brothers Grimm

Retold by Katherine Mattock
Includes:
  The Brave Little Tailor
  The Fisherman and His Wife
  Rapunzel
  The Robber Bridegroom
  Tom Thumb

The Emperor's New Clothes and Other Stories by Hans Christian Andersen

Retold by Janice Tibbetts
Includes:
  The Emperor's New Clothes
  The Brave Tin Soldier
  The Ugly Duckling
  The Nightingale
  The Tinderbox
  The Princess and the Pea

Folk Tales from Around the World

Retold by Rosemary Border
Includes:
  The Pied Piper of Hamelin
  Rip Van Winkle
  The Boy Who Drew Dragons
  Dick Whittington and His Cat
  Where Do Stories Come From?

Heroes and Heroines

Retold by Philip Popescu
Includes:
  Mulan
  William Tell
  Grace Darling
  Robin Hood
  Pocahontas

The Monkey King

Retold by Rosemary Border